*"The story
of life is quicker
than the wink of an eye;
the story of love
is hello and good-bye
until we meet again."*

—Jimi Hendrix

POISONED HEART

I MARRIED DEE DEE RAMONE
(THE RAMONES YEARS)

A PUNK LOVE STORY

BY VERA RAMONE KING

PHOENIX
BOOKS

ISBN-10: 1-59777-612-2
ISBN-13: 978-1-59777-612-7
Library of Congress Cataloging-In-Publication Data Available

Cover Design by: Sonia Fiore
Book Design by: Marti Lou Critchfield & Sonia Fiore

Printed in the United States of America

Phoenix Books, Inc.
9465 Wilshire Boulevard, Suite 840
Beverly Hills, CA 90212

10 9 8 7 6 5 4 3 2 1

Dedicated to Kenny, my husband,
my best friend, my partner....

Without your love, strength, encouragement and total
support this book would not have been written.
Thank you for letting me heal.

TABLE OF CONTENTS

FOREWORD

On October 30, 2008, we had the great pleasure of inducting the Ramones into the Long Island Music Hall of Fame. The Ramones were in good company; the other inductees included Barbra Streisand, Louis Armstrong, Count Basie, Simon and Garfunkel, Aaron Copland, Neil Diamond, Public Enemy, Blue Öyster Cult and folksinger Jean Ritchie. The Ramones are from the borough of Queens, of course, and geographically, Queens and Long Island are where the story of the Ramones began. We felt honored to be asked to induct the Ramones that day, because our bands, Talking Heads and Tom Tom Club, have a long history with those guys.

Our first show ever was opening for the Ramones at CBGB's at the end of May 1975. Our first tour of Europe and the UK during the amazing, exploding heyday of punk rock, in May of 1977, was as support act for the Ramones. We spent long hours on the bus together riding from city to city, and every single show was intensely crazy and wild like we'd never before seen or heard. Now, of all the Ramones, we got to know Dee Dee Ramone best. His curiosity and wonderment were infectious. He became our special pal, joining the two of us on our rare days off, checking out the street art and rock clubs in some of the greatest cities of the world. London! Amsterdam! Paris! Our friend Jerry Harrison, a founding member of the Modern Lovers, who had joined our band just a few months before this, was blown away by Dee Dee. He thought Dee Dee was the "Noble Savage" incarnate!

Our friendship lasted the rest of Dee Dee's life. In 1988, when Tom Tom Club played a fifteen-night stand at CBGB's, we asked Dee Dee to join us onstage for a truly hardcore version of "Psycho Killer." Later on, in 1990, Tom Tom Club toured North America with the Ramones and Debbie Harry on the Escape from New York tour, which for those lucky enough to see it, included, not incidentally, Perry Farrell, of Jane's Addiction and Porno for Pyros. (Perry was inspired by this tour to create his own Lollapalooza tours.) At one point on the Escape from New York tour, CJ Ramone faithfully replaced Dee Dee on bass, which ever after allowed the Ramones to go on with renewed vitality and, just as importantly, allowed Dee Dee to lead a healthier life in which to grow artistically outside of the Ramones. When you read this book, you may begin to understand how the band had become intolerably restrictive for him under the circumstances, as it also had for Tommy Ramone years earlier. After a break, Dee Dee asked to rejoin, but it wasn't to be. Even so, Dee Dee loved the Ramones forever, and he continued to contribute to most of the songs the band would record and play—right to the end.

Through all of his relapses, backsliding, and trips to rehab, Dee Dee remained remarkably productive. One time, our friend, film director Mary Lambert, asked Dee Dee to write a Ramones song for her film version of Stephen King's *Pet Sematary*. Dee Dee agreed and wrote the title song overnight.

I don't want to be buried
In a pet sematary
I don't want to live my life again.

Both Mary and Stephen King loved the song, and it remained in the Ramones repertoire until the end.

Dee Dee was a master of the no-nonsense lyric, as he demonstrated over and over.

In March of 2002, the Ramones and Talking Heads were inducted into the Rock and Roll Hall of Fame. During the ceremony, Dee Dee and CJ Ramone sat with us at our table at the Waldorf Astoria. Dee Dee looked healthy and resplendent in a burgundy sharkskin suit and black Wayfarer shades. Our young sons were in awe of his wit and style. In his acceptance speech, he grinned and literally gave himself a small pat on the back for successfully staying straight for more than a couple of years. Barely two months later, Dee Dee was found dead from an overdose.

There have been a few great punks, but Dee Dee will most likely remain our favorite, not only for his artistry but also for the depth and quality of inner goodness that was present in him, despite his lifelong consuming struggle with inner demons. His demons might have gotten him killed, but they could never destroy his amazingly positive spirit, definitely the greater force.

Some people complained that Dee Dee could be unreliable, and that was certainly true when he was using street drugs. Still, there was always one thing you could count on from Dee Dee: songs, songs, and more great songs. The fact is that Dee Dee Ramone wrote the lion's share of all Ramones songs, even after officially quitting the band. Although Joey, a fantastic singer and frontman, wrote some great songs, too, it's indisputable that Dee Dee was far and away the most prolific songwriter in the band, surely one of the most prolific songwriters of all time. He wrote so many that his friends, Johnny Thunders of the Heartbreakers and Stiv Bators of The Dead Boys, thought he'd never notice if they stole a couple of his songs to pass off as their own. Those punks sure did have some nerve! Dee Dee complained, but they remained friends nevertheless.

From what we know through our experiences with the Ramones, Vera Ramone has written a very accurate portrait of the band, and the first really true and fascinating account of Dee Dee Ramone, the man and the artist. You will read about the strengths and weaknesses of each band member. Her story gives you a very clear picture of what it was like to be a woman in the Ramones' world, and what it was like to be the woman married to Dee Dee. She writes with great understanding and compassion for him and the other Ramones, even though her life with them was alternately chaotic, tiresome, ecstatic, and abusive. Vera doesn't pull her punches, yet she writes without the ego, malice, or self-aggrandizing that so often comes with rock history.

Sharing new information about the band and her life with Dee Dee that has never been publicly disclosed before, Vera will tell you what it was really like to be married to a self-medicating rock star. Dee Dee had suffered from manic depression since he was a teenager, but for many, many years, he didn't have an explanation for his extreme mood swings or know that he could find relief through safe legal treatment. He often felt misunderstood, and Vera gave him understanding. It was through Vera that Dee Dee first found a path to wellness. The story of their love is one of our great modern tragedies. This book tells it all like it was.

When Vera married Dee Dee, everyone who knew them felt that Vera would be a good influence on Dee Dee—without putting bourgeois constraints on him. She was what we call "a cool chick." She was sweet and lovely and hip. Plus, she had a good brain in her head. Doing everything in her power to care for her man and his art, Vera accepted that Dee Dee's demons were as much a part of him as his genius. She worked hard, bringing financial steadiness to their partnership as well as shouldering all their home responsibilities. Like so many women who have dedicated themselves to providing security, affection, and understanding to their very own rock star, she found life to be both a tunnel of love and a house of horrors.

At their wedding, Dee Dee and Vera were dressed in white; rarely have you seen a cuter couple. They got an apartment in Queens not far from Vera's parents, and it looked like life could be beautiful. "*Anything* was possible!" Dee Dee would tell us. How happy, strong, and proud he felt to be living the married life with Vera! He was taking piano lessons and writing a song a day! He was seeing a good doctor, and it was Vera who had helped him turn his life around! We always wondered what went wrong in the troubled times after, especially when Dee Dee didn't mention Vera and his love for her even once in his memoirs. Now Vera gives us some answers to our many questions and clues to others that you, too, might have asked yourself at one point or another.

At least two times that we know of, and probably more, Vera found Dee Dee unconscious and turning blue, and saved his life by calling the paramedics. Vera gave Dee Dee all she could give until one day, nearly too late, she realized that a Dee Dee off his meds would be unsafe to live with, and she had to escape with her own life intact before she could save his. If only she had been there with him on his final day, she might have saved his life again. But Dee Dee had already split and was living a new life, in a new town, thousands of miles away.

There are many "if onlys" that make us wonder if maybe things could have worked out better. Dee Dee was a full-time job for Vera, and often his behavior was more than she and everybody else put together could handle. His addictions and disorders, especially given the prevailing ignorance of the day concerning mental illness, made life a living hell for both of them. And being in a band that was constantly on the road—just so they could pay their rent and eat—made it too complicated for Dee Dee to get the consistent treatment he needed to reverse his habit. The financial hardship of keeping a marginalized, albeit *famous*, band on the road—at a time when most radio stations refused to even play their records—meant that for as long as sales remained poor, as they did through most of the Ramones' working days, virtually their sole means of making a modest living was touring. It would have been extremely hard, if not impossible, for a touring band like the Ramones to provide a more supportive environment for Dee Dee. So conditions remained harsh, considerations for others were scarce, and a narrow militaristic approach to all-things-Ramones-ruled.

It also didn't help that the other Ramones had their own issues with interpersonal relationships. Their idea of team support was "Snap out it," "Pull yourself together," "Life is war," and "To each his own problems." "Tough love" might have been a useful strategy for someone in his earliest stage on the road to recovery, or for somebody who felt loved and understood in childhood, but for Dee Dee and the other Ramones who *never* felt loved enough, tough love was just another form of betrayal. For all of their legendary greatness—and their art is just that—their vision as a unit remained very narrow in focus. Only as individuals were any of the Ramones able to see a way beyond that narrowness, which leaves us with still more "if onlys" concerning the new lives that Joey and Dee Dee especially were beginning to make for themselves when death so suddenly stole them from us.

Dee Dee Ramone wasn't actually using at the time of his death. He'd been clean for a long time. Since losing his good life with Vera, he had finally found some peace and stability once again. He had happily remarried. He was painting and selling pictures, as well as writing songs and performing with his new band. He was cooperating as the fascinating subject of a Mary Lambert documentary (unfinished, unreleased). The warning signs—often quite clear to those who live daily with loved ones afflicted by bipolar disorder—were not apparent to those Dee Dee had asked to join him in his new life. It wasn't their fault, of course, because Dee Dee could suddenly get uncontrollable urges to escape from himself and disappear. In the end, he did not live far from a corner where the dealers did their best to tempt him every single day. His being alone and experiencing an endless moment's desperate need to escape his illness's last attack was all it took to do Dee Dee in—that and an uncontrolled substance taken in a quantity his now-straight body could no longer tolerate. This scenario is so common it's become a rock 'n' roll cliché, which we know, above all, Dee Dee wanted to avoid.

Some people say there is a Ramones curse: first Joey, then Dee Dee, and then Johnny, all gone within a brief few years. Most recently, their friend, champion, and former manager, Linda Stein, was found murdered in her New York apartment. That's a lot of grief for one band and their fans to bear. However powerful the legacy of music they have left, you have to say, "Sure, the music lives on, but that is not much consolation to those who loved them as people and who lost what was most precious to them." Vera and other friends to the Ramones know how amazed and happy Dee Dee, Joey, and Johnny would have been *if only* they had lived to see it all from the perspective of time and distance that we now enjoy. With Vera we can share the true stories of their wild ride and hope we learned something along the way.

Music history records that the Ramones were as much an inspiration to everyone then as they are now. They are an inspiration not just to their talented punk followers, like Green Day, who played a rockin' tribute in true Ramones form at the 2002 Rock and Roll Hall of Fame induction ceremony, but to artists of every ilk and skill, proving that an artist can make something where there was nothing like it before, if only you *drive* yourself to have a positive vision of what can be. All the original members of the Ramones—Joey, Johnny, Tommy, and Dee Dee—along with the true soldiers who stepped in for them—Marky for Tommy and CJ for Dee Dee—were crucial to the chemistry that made up the center of the Ramones team. Still, it's hard to imagine that such a band could have come into being and survived the horrendous situations it endured without special support from a career-long loyal entourage, including the visual artist Arturo Vega, who designed all the Ramones' lighting, logos and T-shirts, and Monte Melnick, their soundman who did double-duty as road manager. You will read here about what an awesome crew they were. At times, the crew and their manager, Gary Kurfirst, when added to the Ramones' unbroken promise to their fans, were all that held the band together.

Just as important to Vera's story, you will learn about the other halves of the Ramones: the moms, girlfriends, and wives who, like Shiva the creator and the destroyer, could cut both ways—literally. For better and for worse, they provided not only life-saving support to their mates, but the love-hate emotional content for a lifetime's supply of Ramones songs. Girls were always a special focus for the lover that was Dee Dee, and his songs never devolved into merely ironic or cynical observation. Forever hiding his feelings in life, in song he expressed them head on, somehow managing to retain all that was essentially vulnerable, confusing, human, and yet proud. Truly childlike and unsophisticated, his songwriting always connected on a deeper level as unfiltered raw emotion. A believer in overcoming the impossible, every song Dee Dee wrote was, for him, a fresh start to a brand new day. And he wrote a new song just about every day.

Vera Ramone has a new and better life these days. Vera is a writer now—and a good one. This book reveals the depth of her feelings. She is going places and, in spite of it all, she still carries Dee Dee in her heart. This book is her special song for Dee Dee. Read on and you will know what we mean. Hey! Ho! Let's Go!

— Chris Frantz and Tina Weymouth,
November 14, 2008

CHAPTER ONE

The Beginning

I arrived into this world on a hot August afternoon in Manhattan in 1953. My parents, John and Rose Boldis, had high hopes and dreams for my future. They were both of Slovakian descent and met in New York City after the war in the early 1950s; my father was still in the army at the time. My mother was only twenty when they got married, and the following year, they had me. Being the eldest of five children and raised in a strict Catholic household, I had many responsibilities growing up. I was "expected" to set a good example for my younger siblings and was never allowed to be less than the perfect child. If I got an A minus, why wasn't it an A? No matter what I did, nothing seemed good enough.

I can remember back as early as when I was nine and ten years old, immersing myself in music. I grew up watching *American Bandstand* religiously and could count down the Top 10 every week with Cousin Brucie. Music was my escape, the one thing I truly loved. The first concert I ever went to see was when the Beatles performed at Shea Stadium. I was only twelve years old, but that experience totally changed my life. My love for music and for musicians became an obsession for me from that point on.

I attended an all-girl Catholic grade school, but it was clear from the start that I had a wild streak in me. I was a bit of a wild child. At school we all had to wear boring plaid uniforms with knee-highs, white blouses, and these silly little bow ties and berets. I had wanted to wear my new pair of mod shoes, which were very cool at the time, but they just didn't look right with the knee-highs, so I wore them to school with a pair of black sheer stockings. Not surprisingly, I was sent home at lunchtime to change. Another time, I remember one nun taking me into the hall and washing the makeup off of my face. Since my hair was teased, she proceeded to put my head under the sink faucet as well. Afterwards, I was sent home early.

Several weeks later I went to school wearing my new white go-go boots with my uniform plaid skirt rolled up. Eventually, my parents were called up to school to meet with the principal. It wasn't like I was trying to provoke anyone; I was simply expressing myself and who I was. Well, this did not sit well with the Catholic nuns. After the seventh grade we moved, and I started public school—I liked this so much better!

During my high school years, I continued to develop my unique sense of style and worked at an upscale boutique in Flushing, Queens, named Ronnies. There was another branch located in Forest Hills, and both stores were known for having the coolest clothes, handbags, shoes, and makeup. And they always played the best music. Every week, I would spend almost my entire paycheck on the latest fashions, which I would put aside as soon as they arrived in the store. Among my friends and at school, I was known as the girl who had the best clothes, handbags, and shoes. I was always coordinated and put-together. Style came naturally to me and was just the beginning of something that played a major part in who I was becoming as a person.

As a youngster I idolized women like Twiggy, Pattie Boyd, Marianne Faithful, Anita Pallenberg, Jane

Asher, Cynthia Lennon, and Jean Shrimpton. I tried to emulate their looks with the heavy eyeliner, white lipstick, and long straight hair and bangs—the whole London mod look—but I was only twelve at the time. In my strict Catholic household, there was only so far I could get with white go-go boots, Hullabaloo sweatshirts, and rolled-up skirts. A lot of boys liked me, but my parents ran the family with an iron hand, and I dared not go against them. Although I was only sixteen or seventeen, going to clubs was another of my favorite pastimes, and I'd have to borrow my friends' IDs to get in. Overall my teen years were a blast— I wouldn't change one second.

I was barely eighteen when I abruptly left home one day to find myself and figure out what I wanted out of life. The 1960s and early 1970s were a tumultuous time for raising kids—keeping the family focused took a lot of hard work and patience—and my leaving left my parents totally heartbroken. After a brief marriage of my own and being disowned by my mom and dad, I returned home at twenty-two to make peace with my parents and try to be the perfect daughter again. By day I worked in the Garment Center answering phones and modeling clothes for the manufacturers, but at night I went to the city and explored the underground music scene that was so exciting in the 1970s. Little did I know that somewhere across the big pond was the man of my dreams.

* * *

Douglas Glenn Colvin was born on September 18, 1952, in Fort Lee, Virginia. His father, Glenn, was in the army and stationed in Germany when he met Dee Dee's mother, Toni. She was only eighteen years old and working as a dancer at the Scala in Berlin when she met this handsome, older American military man. A short time later, they moved back to the states, where they married and had Douglas. As an infant, he was taken to Tokyo, Japan, and less than a year later they relocated and were stationed in Berlin, where he was raised.

Douglas (Dee Dee) was an army brat. He had a lot of fun growing up in Germany, but his was a dysfunctional family. This led to his parents splitting up by the time he was about fourteen years old. After their separation, his mother took him and his sister, Beverly, back to the states where they eventually settled in Forest Hills, Queens, in the mid-1960s. Forest Hills was an upper-middle class neighborhood, where Dee Dee encountered a lot of rich, snooty, spoiled brats. After the divorce, his father moved to Atlanta, Georgia, and his mother struggled as a single parent trying her best to raise two children on her own. These were hard times!

Toni worked at Gimbels department store during the day, and in the evenings she took cosmetology classes. Eventually, she got a job working at the prestigious Elizabeth Arden Salon on Fifth Ave. in New York City. While she was working day and night to give her family a good life, there admittedly wasn't much supervision at home. There was no father figure, or any other kind of male influence, in Dee Dee's life during these crucial years—someone who could give him the guidance and sense of direction he so desperately needed.

Before long, Dee Dee started to hang with the wrong crowd and began to run wild. He absolutely hated school and instead of going to class, Dee Dee would spend most of his days drinking beer with his friends or going to sniff glue in someone's basement. By the time he was sixteen he begged his mother to sign him out of school. She didn't want to, but he convinced her into believing that he'd be better off working. She knew he wasn't going to school anyway, but agreed with much hesitation. Finally Dee Dee had the freedom he had been craving. Toni realized that she didn't have any control over him at this point, no matter how hard she tried, so she continued to indulge and focus all of her attention on his sister Beverly, who dreamed of becoming a professional ballerina.

Meanwhile, Dee Dee was left to fend for himself, and shortly after this, he moved out of the house and befriended John Cummings (Johnny) and Jeff Hyman (Joey). Even though they had known each other from around the neighborhood, they started hanging out when Dee Dee was sixteen. Not one of them was going to school, and all three were obsessed with the idea of starting their own rock band. The only drawback was that none of the three boys could play a single instrument—and this was a problem.

His mother told me that at about this time something happened to Dee Dee. He changed from a sweet, sensitive young boy into an entirely different person. She often wondered if it was then that he began using drugs. Toni had tried to be the best mother she could under the circumstances, but she was particularly hurt, embarrassed, and distraught at the way her son later portrayed her in his book, *Lobotomy*. She didn't deserve to be portrayed in such a negative, untrue way. Dee Dee wrote that book out of sheer anger, and it left his mother totally devastated.

After he quit school, Dee Dee took on a variety of different jobs. He first worked as a butcher's apprentice, then as a salesman in an electronics store, and also as a stock boy at a local supermarket. It was in the basement of this supermarket that Dee Dee was first introduced to heroin. In the beginning he disliked the drug—it made him nauseous—but he tried heroin again because the guys at work made such a big deal about it. Finally, he felt cool, like he really fit in. It wasn't long before he went from snorting heroin to shooting it on a regular basis. After Joey's parents kicked him out of the house, he and Dee Dee started sleeping in the back of a paint store in Forest Hills owned by Joey's mother. They were still constantly fantasizing about being rock stars. But Dee Dee didn't want to grow up to be a bum, so he got a job working as a mail clerk for an ad agency in Manhattan. It was during this time that they all met Tommy Erdelyi, who was a couple of years older and hung out in clubs like Max's Kansas City and Nobody's in Manhattan.

However far apart Dee Dee was from his mother, during his lean times she would always give him her last dollar. Even after he had moved out of the house, she would go out of her way to indulge him with all of his favorite things. Every Sunday he would bring his laundry to her apartment in Forest Hills, and she would have his favorite German meal cooked for him. Sundays were always their day together. This continued for many years—even after Dee Dee and I were married, we would still always spend Sundays with his mom.

CHAPTER TWO

The Ramones are Born

It was in the early 1970s when people like Alice Cooper, Lou Reed, David Bowie, and Mick Jagger would be seen hanging out in the strictly V.I.P.-only back room of New York City club Max's Kansas City. Tommy Ramone was the one who turned Dee Dee, Johnny, and Joey onto this hip scene, where the glitter look was really in. The look was all about huge three-inch platform shoes, skintight clothes, glamorous ruffled shirts with rhinestones and sequins, shag hairdos, and rainbow-colored afros. The soon-to-be Ramones did not look like that at all. They wore dirty blue jeans with holes in them, old worn-out T-shirts, and sneakers—they looked like punks! It wasn't long after the guys started hanging out at these New York City clubs that Dee Dee bought his first pair of snakeskin boots. He also had his hair done and started dressing up, trying to emulate the look that dominated the scene, but that just wasn't him.

Seeing legendary bands like the New York Dolls and the infamous, and outrageous, Iggy Pop and the Stooges was what inspired these four punks from Queens to start their own band. Unfortunately not one of the four could play an instrument, and they definitely couldn't afford expensive equipment, so with their fifty-dollar guitars and tiny little amps they practiced and wrote short, loud, and rough songs. At first Dee Dee was the singer, Joey was the drummer, and Johnny was trying to play the guitar.

Everything changed when it became apparent that Dee Dee should play the bass; Joey just tore up the drum kits, so he became the singer; Tommy was originally their manager and ended up being the band's drummer; and Johnny kept on trying to play the guitar. They could only play a few chords, at best, which resulted in the harshest sounds. They were hostile and had bad attitudes so the music that came out of them became known as punk rock.

At first they started rehearsing only a few hours a week, which is how they got their unique raw sound. Even after scraping several songs together, the Ramones' sets still lasted about twenty minutes. Because they weren't yet rock and roll stars, the boys kept their day jobs. At the time, Dee Dee was an assistant hairdresser at the Bergdorf Goodman salon where he shampooed the heads of mostly older women. Johnny kept working for his dad in construction, Tommy was a roadie for Buzzy Linhart, and Joey was just, well, Joey.

It was Dee Dee who came up with the name "the Ramones" after reading in a music magazine that Paul McCartney would often use the alias "Paul Ramone" during the Silver Beatles Tour. Douglas Glenn Colvin, a huge McCartney fan, referred to himself as Dee Dee Ramone. The rest of the band quickly adapted the "Ramone" surname, too, just to make things simpler. It would be easier for the fans to remember them that way even though none of them were actually brothers. Soon the band started calling itself the Ramones, and so the Ramones were born!

After deciding on a band name, the Ramones also had to establish a style of dress. Black leather motorcycle jackets, torn jeans, and sneakers quickly became their image of choice. As far as the songwriting went, they had no choice: they wrote their own songs because they couldn't figure out how to perform covers! As far as I know, the first Ramones' original was "I Don't Wanna Walk Around With You." Most of their early songs had similar titles: "I Don't Wanna Go Down To The Basement," "I Wanna Be Well," "Now I Wanna Sniff Some Glue," and "I Don't Care." These songs were all written from their real-life experiences. I think it was Joey who wrote "Beat On The Brat" when he lived in the Birchwood Towers in Forest Hills.

The first time they played a showcase was at Performance Studios in Manhattan. By this point they had already acquired their signature eagle backdrop designed by Arturo Vega. The logo was a presidential seal with the eagle holding a baseball bat in one hand and an arrow in the other. Arturo Vega was the band's artistic director and later became their lighting manager and primary merchandiser, selling and making all Ramones T-shirts and swag. Arturo was very smart and dependable and was part of the extended family that lasted until the very end.

During these early years, Joey and Dee Dee lived at Arturo's big loft which was only a couple of doors down from the legendary, and now defunct, music venue, Country Blue Grass and Blues, affectionately known as CBGB's by music-lovers worldwide. CBGB's had a dank, old, long room with a bar on the right-hand side and sawdust on the floor. As Tommy once said, there was nowhere else to play at the time *but* CBGB's, so they started doing shows there regularly. In fact, one of the Ramones' first shows at the infamous New York City music spot was when they opened for Blondie, who was known as Angel and the Snake at that time.

It took a while before the Ramones finally got their first official gig at CBGB's, where they played the real loud and fast songs "Now I Wanna Sniff Some Glue," "Beat On The Brat," "Lobotomy," "I Wanna Be Your Boyfriend," and "Blitzkrieg Bop." During their early live performances, the audience would just be getting into the music, about twenty minutes into the set, when suddenly it was over, before it barely even got started! The energy that came out of the Ramones was unique, to say the least. The kids in the crowd would just stare at each other like, *What was that? What just happened?* Well, whatever happened was so fast and loud that it left everyone wanting more. I'll always remember the first time I saw Dee Dee up there onstage, and instantly picked him out as my favorite Ramone. He was so-o-o cute, and he had such a special style and charisma about him. Dee Dee was definitely the sexiest Ramone.

The following flyer was sent out in 1974 under the heading "The Ramones":

The Ramones are not an oldies group, they are not a glitter group, they don't play boogie music and they don't play the blues. The Ramones are an original Rock and Roll group of 1974, and their songs are brief, to the point and everyone a potential hit single. The quartet consists of Johnny, Joey, Dee Dee and Tommy Ramone. Johnny, the guitarist plays with such force that his sound has been compared to a hundred howitzers going off. Joey the lead singer, is an arch villain who's lanky frame stands threatening center stage. Dee Dee is base [sic] guitar and the acknowledged handsome one of the group, and Tommy is the drummer, pulsating, playing launches and [the] throbbing sound of the band.

The Ramones' legend and myth had begun.

It was while they were playing at CBGB's that Craig Leon, the PR man for Sire Records, saw them for the first time. Slowly, the Ramones began to sell out all their shows, and lines gathered around the block to get in. By this time Craig had convinced Seymour Stein, the president of Sire Records, to come down to CBGB's to see them play. Punk rock might have never hit America if not for the iconic Seymour Stein, who was brilliant enough to recognize and envision the potential of something as new, raw, and exciting as the Ramones. It was Seymour who was able to see outside of the box, so to speak, and take a risk on these four young punks from Forest Hills, Queens. He knew they had something *different* about them, something unique and original, and he was right. The Ramones and fellow CBGB bands, like the Debbie Harry-led Blondie, New Wave innovators The Talking Heads, and "Godmother of Punk" Patti Smith, became part of the "Bowery Phenomenon." Soon after signing the Ramones to his label, Seymour gave the foursome their first recording contract. The Ramones were ecstatic. It was a dream come true for the four punks from Queens, and they just couldn't believe their luck. Their first album only cost $6,000 to record and put Tommy, Johnny, Joey, and Dee Dee on the map and their road to destiny, eventually ending at the Rock and Roll Hall of Fame.

Their first trip to London, England, was in 1976 where they played at the Roundhouse on the Fourth of July. This was the steamiest and most exciting night the Ramones had experienced to date—nothing short of a punk explosion to the ultimate degree. It was at the Roundhouse where future bands like the Sex Pistols, Siouxsie and the Banshees, The Clash, The Buzzcocks, and others saw the Ramones for the first time and decided right then and there that they were going to be in a band.

The Ramones were the pioneers and true fathers of punk rock. There was no one like them, then or since. They became quintessential legends over night.

But as hard as they worked and as many live shows as they performed in, they couldn't get any kind of radio airplay. A DJ would get fired if he strayed from the designated format, playing REO Speedwagon, Styx, and Billy Joel. Some college stations could get away with playing punk rock or some radio stations played an hour a week of what they called "New Wave Hour." Vince Scelsa from WNEW in New York often played the Ramones on his Sunday morning show. He ended up being a big fan. Long Island's WLIR, hosted by Denis McNamara, the station's general manager, allowed "alternative rock," and the Ramones would often win the title "Screamer of the Week," where the general audience would call in and vote for their favorite group. One morning at 8:00 a.m., DJ Ben Manilla called Dee Dee just to wish him a Happy Birthday from WLIR and all his fans. Dee Dee loved that—and it turned out to be the start of a great day for him.

Before long, the Ramones were playing CBGB's, the Mercer Arts Theater, and Max's Kansas City on a regular basis. Also on the bill were bands like Blondie, the Talking Heads, Television, Jayne County, and Patti Smith, just to name a few of the acts that began to emerge on this new, hip underground scene.

CHAPTER THREE

My New Boyfriend

In late November 1977, I returned home from a trip to Florida with my best friends Regina and Carole. It was in Miami that I was introduced to rock star Rod Stewart—my friends and I had just attended his concert—and Rod and I went on a couple of dates before I had to return to New York, and Rod had to continue on with his tour. A few nights later, back in New York, I went to Max's Kansas City and met Dee Dee Ramone for the first time. I was standing at the bar when he walked in and stood next to me. To my surprise we had both ordered the same drink, blackberry brandy on the rocks. It was cold outside and not a common drink. He started talking to me and kept telling me his name was Dee Dee. Of course, I recognized who he was, but I chose not to look impressed.

I found him very charming, funny, and extremely good-looking. There was something special about him. I fell in love with his deep hearty laugh, big brown eyes, and shy, rather bashful demeanor. He was quite unique and captivating in his own way, which was all very appealing and exciting to me. He spoke in a raspy, yet distinct voice that really turned me on. I thought he was gorgeous, and especially since he was a rocker, as far as I was concerned, Dee Dee had the whole package. I was totally hooked, and I guess he was hooked too, because Dee Dee often told me—and various interviewers—that for him, it was love at first sight. That first night we hung out and chatted for several hours and had a great time. He took my number and said he was leaving for England in the next few days with the Ramones but that he'd call me when he returned to the states. Since he was leaving the country, I wasn't really sure that I would actually hear from him again. To my surprise, I came home from work one day, and my mother told me a "Dee Dee" had called for me from England and that he would try again later. I was so excited I just wanted to sit by the phone and wait for it to ring. He called again the next day and told me he would be coming back home soon and that he would like to see me again. I literally counted the days—hours!—until we would meet again.

Dee Dee had quite a reputation. I knew he'd had several girlfriends and was known as quite the ladies' man. I'd even remembered reading about him on the walls of CBGB's bathrooms! During one of his first calls to me, I heard a girl screaming at him and beating him up as she dragged him out of the phone booth. I later found out that it had been Patti Giordano, a waitress at Max's Kansas City, with whom he had been staying when he met me.

Ironically, I was seeing legendary rock photographer Bob Gruen, who was also seeing Patti Giordano, although we didn't know it then. Bob was well known for his photos and was a good friend of John Lennon, as well as the punk rock group the New York Dolls. So here Bob, Patti, Dee, and I were: The Bob, Carol, Ted and Alice of rock and roll. One day I finally told Bob that I was seeing Dee Dee, and he admitted to me that he was also seeing Patti. I think the four of us were in shock when the news came out. Regardless, we all remained close. To this day, Bob and I are still good friends after thirty years of knowing each other. Both Dee Dee and Patti have passed on, from an overdose and AIDS respectively.

After Dee Dee returned home from England he stayed at the loft owned by his manager, Danny Fields. By this point, Patti had thrown him out. Ever since that very first day we became joined at the hip and were soon very much in love with one another. We quickly became punk's royal couple, the alternative to the Sid and Nancy image. With me, Dee Dee was always so sweet and kind and loving; we held hands everywhere we went. In our early days, I was very naïve and didn't know any addicts, so for almost two years Dee Dee was able to keep his heroin addiction from me. When I found out, I was, expectedly, totally crushed.

One of my good memories from the time was when Betsy Johnson approached me at Max's Kansas City to tell me she loved my look and style and to ask if I would take part in a photo shoot she was doing. The now very famous and recognizable fashion designer was not well known then, but my friend Regina and I went anyway. It turned out to be a ton of fun. Another punk designer with her own boutique on St. Mark's Place, Natasha, became my personal stylist. She designed one-of-a-kind punk rock clothes for me and also became a good friend. I modeled in several punk fashion shows for her cable TV program and in a fashion show at the trendy Peppermint Lounge.

CHAPTER FOUR

Life in the Punk Lane

Soon after New Year's 1978 I was to embark on my first Ramones tour, which started in Los Angeles. The opening act was the Runaways, featuring a sixteen-year-old Joan Jett and Lita Ford, who I found out later had a major crush on Dee Dee. At this time things were definitely financially tough for us. Dee Dee made only one hundred dollars a week, and the two of us lived on ten dollars per diem for food. His heroin addiction alone cost one hundred dollars a day, and typically that much money would only buy him two Tuinals and a beer—at the most. These were lean times for Dee Dee and me, to say the least.

It was during the Ramones' three-month-long 1978 tour that an incident occurred that I will never forget. We were in Tulsa, Oklahoma, the heart of the Bible Belt, and at four o'clock in the afternoon on a Saturday, we were shocked to find every store in town was already closed. The Ramones had a show that night, and we were curious as to how many punks would actually come to the show, if there were any fans at all in this part of the country, or was it going to be a bomb? Surprisingly, the show went much better than we all had hoped, but what happened next was slightly more disconcerting.

As we were all exiting the venue into the parking lot and walking towards the van, with rain pouring down and thunder and lightning striking menacingly in the distance, a sinister young man approached us. He was dressed in a long, black leather coat and hat, clutching a bible in one hand and a cross in the other, and had a group of followers behind him. Suddenly, he started preaching to the band, telling them to change their evil ways and condemned punk music and everything associated with it. He approached each member of the Ramones individually, wanting to "save them from themselves" and ranting on and on about how they should repent for the sake of saving their souls and change their devil-worshipping ways. "Repent or die! You must change your wicked ways or you will be cursed for life!" he screamed as we approached the van. Behind him, his followers were praying aloud and repeating the preacher's every word, cursing our very souls for denouncing God, and cursing each and every member of the band as we all piled into the van. If there ever was such a thing as a curse, this was it. It truly felt like a night from hell. Finally, after his pleas were ignored, falling on deaf ears, and we were all safely in the van, Johnny said to Monte, "Monte, get this fucking nut outta here!"

We just laughed it off at the time—"What a bunch of weirdo nut jobs," "Let's get the hell outta here!"—but the van got silent as we drove away. Obviously, we were all affected by what we had just witnessed. It was a very eerie and bizarre experience—even Dee Dee said that preacher had given him the creeps. No one spoke until we reached the nearest convenience store to get some treats to bring back to the hotel with us. (This was a ritual every night after the show, to stock up on snacks.)

The night had ended on an extremely profound note. I think we all wondered, *Was this curse for real?* After Joey and Dee Dee had passed away, and I knew Johnny was real sick, I wondered if that young guy had actually put some kind of curse on them. *Was that even possible?* It certainly was ironic and uncanny that as soon as all three of them reached the age of fifty, they were on a quick decline as though they were living on borrowed time. I often wonder how it happened that three such wonderful people—Joey, Dee Dee, and Johnny Ramone— could have left us so suddenly and within a short time of each other. They were so young and didn't even get a chance to enjoy the legacy they'd left behind. Now would have been their time to enjoy life after working hard for so many years, but almost in the blink of an eye, they were gone. They are very missed, and they still live through their music and their loyal fans. Who would have thought that their music would have been heard by three generations and that they would be more popular today than they were then? They may have left us physically, but their music will live on for many years to come. This is my main reason for having written this book—to keep Dee Dee's legacy alive.

Yes, he was difficult, but he was also kind, loving, sweet, generous, and very funny. He had a wonderful sense of humor about himself and always had a deep, wonderful distinctive laugh. To know the real Dee Dee was to love him. Through the good times, the bad, and the ugly, Dee Dee was a special person. If a man is touched by genius, he is not an ordinary person. He does not lead an ordinary life. *That* was the Dee Dee I knew and fell in love with, and I want his fans to know and remember him in this same way. He spoke through his lyrics and music, and if you listen to his songs, you can hear him and his messages. One does not live life and not know heartache, sorrow, and pain. Few are privileged to know true love and eternal happiness. I hope he has found his nirvana, and his soul is at peace. A lot of people walk through your life but few leave footprints on your heart. One can only wonder whether that curse could have had some validity to it. This was, and has continued to be, quite disturbing to me throughout these last few years. I guess we can only speculate, but we'll never know the answer.

Not long after the tour with The Runaways, Tommy had had enough. The touring—all nine of us piled into a Chevy van—was back to back, nonstop, day after day, sometimes lasting three months or longer at a stretch, and Tommy couldn't take it any longer. He was this-close to having a nervous breakdown. His leaving was a huge disappointment for the band. He was an integral part of the Ramones' history, and without his direction the band might have never come to fruition. Replacing an original member of the group like Tommy was going to be difficult. But as luck would have it, Mark Bell (formerly of Dust, Richard Hell and the Void Oids, and Jayne County) was asked to join the Ramones. He was a perfect fit. Right away Marky Ramone stepped in, and the Ramones continued their insane schedule after only a few short rehearsals. It was back to business as usual.

It was during this time and for several years to follow that Dee Dee's old girlfriend Connie, who was a heroin junkie and prostitute, would constantly show up at gigs. She knew Dee Dee and I were serious and in love and tried every dirty trick in the book to break us up. At one point, Connie was frequenting the Odyssey House (the rehab center where Dee Dee was an outpatient) pretending to be me and using *my* name to try to get in to see Dee Dee, only to be thrown out because they knew of her and that she was constantly harassing us in any way she could. While driving home after rehearsals, Dee Dee would actually crouch down in the van when he would see her hooking for ten-dollar tricks on the streets in the Bowery. He often told me how bad she looked, and how he would sometimes have to run to get away from her. He would avoid Connie and hide every time he got a glimpse of her. I remember reading a statement that another girlfriend of his had made after Dee Dee and I broke up, saying Dee Dee's happiest years were spent with Connie. Ha, ha, what a joke! Connie was a stalker, and a violent one at that. The only hold she had over Dee Dee was supplying him with heroin for the brief amount of time they were together, because he was hooked. Their relationship was based on drugs, not love.

Dee Dee told me about how, one time, she walked into their apartment and found him in bed with Nancy Spungen. Connie was such a violent person that she physically attacked Dee Dee with a broken beer bottle and jammed it into his buttocks. He had a huge scar on his ass for the rest of his life from that horrific relationship, just because she had caught him cheating on her. Connie was a pathetic person, and stalker to boot. The only way she could hold on to any man was to supply him with heroin. Another time her former boyfriend, Arthur Kane from the New York Dolls (pre-Dee Dee), went all the way to Florida to try to get away from her. She followed him there, where they got into such a horrible fight that Arthur grabbed her breast and ripped out her breast implant. After that, she only had one boob to hustle with and make money.

Once Connie tried to crash my birthday party at Max's Kansas City, and the owners had to call the police to have her thrown out. I remember that New York Dolls' David Johansen, who was at our table that night, saw me becoming completely agitated by Connie's harassment. He told me not to let her overwhelm me, that she had nothing on me so not to worry, and that she was just a washed-up old hooker still living in the past. She was a persistent pain in the ass and became another reason why we eventually moved out of the city to the quiet suburb of Whitestone, Queens. You knew she had to be a nutjob for even Dee Dee to be afraid of her—and he was! She was like a bad cold, and no matter what you did she kept coming back. Like gum on your shoe, you just couldn't get rid of her no matter how hard you tried. When Dee Dee eventually left her for good he wrote the song "Glad to See You Go"—he most definitely was. Not long after our encounters with Connie, she was found dead of an overdose in a tenement downtown somewhere in the Bowery.

During the spring of 1978 I lived with Dee Dee and the legendary Danny Fields at his loft on Chambers Street and Broadway. By then I was always with Dee Dee anyway and never at home. Living at Danny Fields' loft was great. He was always sweet to me, a super nice guy, and very balanced. He was quite knowledgeable and always gave thoughtful advice to a good friend. I was busy working in Brooklyn at a hair salon, not making much money but trying to save what I could so Dee Dee and I could venture out on our own. I didn't want to take advantage of Danny's generous hospitality, so I had been keeping a small wad of savings in my drawer in the room that Dee Dee and I shared. One day I came home to find the money was missing, and Dee Dee told me a story, which I later found out was a complete lie.

He said a friend of Danny's from New Jersey— who was staying at the loft around the same time as we were—had stolen the money to get high. Later I learned it was Dee Dee *and* Danny's friend who had taken my hard-earned savings and copped dope while I was at work. A week or so later we found out that Danny's friend, who beyond this incident always seemed like a nice kid, had gone home to New Jersey for the weekend and hung himself at his parents' home in their backyard shed. He didn't even seem depressed when we lived with him, and he was always quite pleasant actually. Danny took the news hard, as we all did. It was so sad and devastating and just didn't seem to make any sense.

Regardless of how the money disappeared, this series of events put me back at square one (although I learned my lesson: I carried my money around with me at all times from then on). Unlike a lot of the other band members' girls I was not a dancer or a hooker. I had a real 9-to-5 job, and although it didn't pay too well, at least it was an honest day's work. No matter how hard I worked, saving for a month's rent and security at $2.25 an hour was a never-ending struggle.

One morning at Danny's, I woke up and decided to make myself a cup of tea. Danny was already out, Dee Dee was still sleeping, and it was quiet in the house. While I was sitting at the kitchen table I noticed a postcard from some exotic faraway island like Martinique, and I flipped it over. The note read something like, "Dear Danny, We're having a wonderful time here with the family away from everything. Hope to see you soon, Linda, Paul, Heather, Mary and Stella." I realized immediately that this was a postcard from Linda and Paul McCartney and their family. There I was, holding a postcard from my idol— one of the Beatles! Danny had many celebrity friends over all the time: The Bay City Rollers, Sean Cassidy, Linda and Paul McCartney, and so many more. I had grown up reading *16 Magazine*, of which he was editor-in-chief. That was my bible growing up! I never in my wildest dreams thought I'd be living in Danny's house, much less consider him a personal friend. He was a wonderful inspiration to many and deserves to be recognized for all of his accomplishments in the music business.

After the tour ended with the Runaways, while we were living with Danny, Dee Dee and I decided to officially get engaged. We went to the Diamond District somewhere around 47th Street and found the perfect pear-shaped diamond ring, which Dee Dee proudly put on my finger. Luckily we had just received a check from his accountant, Ira Herzog, from the previous tour, otherwise we wouldn't have been able to afford it. But no matter how little money we had, Dee Dee insisted on buying an engagement ring, which truly solidified our connection and made it real.

One of my favorite memories from the early days of my relationship with Dee Dee happened while we were staying at Danny's, and I had gotten sick with the flu. Dee Dee decided he was going to cook something for me. I was running a high fever at this time and thought it was so kind of Dee Dee, even though it was slightly out of his character. I tried to tell him I wasn't hungry, but he insisted on making some sort of oatmeal or farina to help me get better. He was so sweet and proudly brought me this huge bowl with a big spoon in it. He had to go to some promo event that night, so I just put the bowl under the bed after he left—I didn't have much of an appetite.

The next day, I was straightening up the room when I pulled out my "Dee Dee Special." To our amazement the spoon was standing straight up in the bowl, the contents of which were as hard as cement. We burst out laughing as Dee Dee turned the bowl over holding just the spoon. The spoon actually became part of the bowl! We threw it out, and Dee Dee let me handle the cooking after that, which was just fine with me.

Near the end of April, I brought Dee Dee home to meet my parents for the first time. This had given him so much anxiety that he overmedicated himself as usual. Things seemed to be going well, though, until he fell off a barstool in my parent's basement. At this point my dad took me over to the side and told me that Dee Dee was in no condition to go back to Manhattan and that he was welcome to spend the night downstairs on the pull-out couch. So the first night Dee Dee met my family, he ended up staying the night, and I was relieved that he didn't have to travel back to the city from Queens. My parents gradually got to know him over the next few months, and by the time our wedding day arrived, that September, they had welcomed him into the family, despite our many problems. Dee Dee was the man I had chosen to spend the rest of my life with, and they accepted him unconditionally but knew it was going to be a long, hard road ahead for the both of us.

Shortly afterwards, we were able to get a little two-bedroom, one-garage apartment in Whitestone, Queens. Dee Dee and I didn't have much, but we did manage to buy a bedroom set, although we still had lawn furniture in the living room. We absolutely loved having our own place and enjoyed our new home, even though we spent a lot of time on the road. When we were not traveling with the band, we were able to spend time in our new apartment and started to adapt to the daily routines and structure of a real home life.

In June of 1978, right after we moved into our Whitestone place, Dee Dee woke up early one morning, and I noticed that he didn't look right. He seemed very weak and was sweating profusely. When I took his temperature, the thermometer read 104 degrees. Immediately we took him to the doctor, and soon after, he was admitted to Parsons Hospital in Flushing, Queens, and diagnosed with Hepatitis B. A few days later, Dee Dee was sent home to rest, and I was also injected with the antidote for the Hepatitis B virus. Little did I know that I had already been infected. We were told Hep B could only be contacted through intravenous needles or sexual contact. We both knew how Dee Dee got the virus—his heroin addiction—so our main focus became getting him well again. It was no surprise that I had contracted the virus from Dee Dee. In those early years it was not unusual for us to have sex five times a day. Ever since the day we met, we were extremely sexually attracted to one another. This earned Dee Dee the nickname I had for him, "Bunny." In return, mine was "Bunness." We had several other pet names for one another, as many couples do.

As soon as we got Dee Dee's diagnosis, I called Monte, the Ramones' road manager, so he could inform the band that Dee Dee was really sick and would be bedridden for a while. Within hours Dee Dee received a phone call from Johnny Ramone informing him that he *had* to play a gig that upcoming Friday night and that was that. Dee Dee couldn't even stand he was so sick and weak. But Johnny would not bend. He refused to cancel the show due to Dee Dee's illness. Needless to say, I was furious that anyone could be so mean and coldhearted. Johnny couldn't have cared less if Dee Dee were to drop dead playing onstage that night. He insisted that the show must go on. There would be no cancellations. *That was that!*

Just two days later, Monte picked him up and took him to play at a local gig (local, meaning they were close enough to drive home after the show and did not have to stay overnight at a hotel). For the love of God, I don't know how Dee Dee performed the show that night with a temperature of 103. But he just couldn't stand up to Johnny, despite the doctor's warnings that there would be dire consequences if he did not rest and overheated his body. It could have pushed him over the edge. This did not sit well with me, and I let Johnny know how I felt. I was definitely getting to know the real John by this time, and it was always his way or no way. Johnny was the self-appointed boss of the band and treated the others as though they were mere employees of his company. Joey, Dee Dee, and Marky didn't stand a fighting chance against John no matter what their personal opinions were.

This didn't only pertain to Dee Dee; Johnny also made Joey play no matter how sick he was, with the flu or for other reasons, and the same went for Marky. He never treated Marky as an equal member of the band, even after so many years. It was so unfair, but there was nothing that could be said or done to change John's way of thinking. When the Ramones fired Danny Fields and Linda Stein, it was John's choice ultimately, but he tried to blame it on us girls, saying that we had put the guys up to it. It was all a big cover-up so John didn't have to look like the bad guy. We had nothing to say about Danny and Linda getting fired whatsoever; in reality, it was all about who could make them more money. Eventually they hired Gary Kurfirst at Overland Productions, who became the Ramones' manager for a good fifteen years. The guys had always worked their asses off, but at least with Gary they finally had something to show for it. Gary also managed other popular bands at that time, like the Talking Heads, Blondie, the B-52's, the Eurythmics, and others, and often arranged for several of his groups to play on the same bill.

Finally, on Saturday, September 2, 1978, Dee Dee and I were married. Our wedding was to be a small affair, about seventy people or so, just close friends and family. Two days before the wedding Dee Dee's friend and best man, Joel Tornebenne, flew from Los Angeles to New York on a private jet and took Dee Dee back with him to the West Coast for a private bachelor party. Joel's high-society girlfriend Carolyn Zecca, my sister Sonja, and my best friend Regina celebrated my bachelorette party with me out on the town, hitting up New York City's Studio 54 and Xenon clubs. Then when Friday night came, the whole wedding party met at the church of St. John Nepomucene at 1st Avenue and 68th Street in New York City for the rehearsal. I remember Father George, the priest who married us, giving Dee Dee and I an intense speech on fidelity, trust, and keeping true to our hearts. We certainly didn't look like the average young couple getting married in a Catholic Church.

The day of the ceremony was nerve-wracking to say the least. I remember someone telling me that Dee Dee might be too stoned to even show up! The mere thought of that happening made me cringe with anxiety— I hoped that my dream wedding would not turn into a nightmare. Fortunately, the day was beautiful, and I arrived in a white Rolls-Royce with my father, fashionably late. As I walked down the aisle and saw Dee Dee standing there waiting at the altar for me, I realized *our* dream was coming true. Soon we would be Mr. and Mrs. Douglas Colvin, and we were ecstatic!

Our reception was catered and held in an outdoor garden at a popular restaurant called the Villa Bianca in

Queens. The whole band was there except for Johnny. Besides Joey Ramone and Tommy Ramone, there were Arturo Vega, Monte A. Melnick, Linda and Seymour Stein, and Danny Fields, among other guests. Johnny didn't come because he thought Dee Dee was making a big mistake. He said Dee Dee was not stable enough to be married, and he thought that it would be bad for the band's image to have Dee Dee, the heartthrob of the Ramones, married. Plus, Johnny was going through a divorce from his first wife Rosanna, so he was not keen on the whole idea of marriage at the time.

Naturally, I saw things differently. In this case I gave Dee Dee stability, a good home life, lots of love and care, and most of all the support he needed during his long struggle for sobriety from alcohol and drug abuse. From my perspective, I had married and fallen in love with the man of my dreams. I was on cloud nine. And in marrying me, Dee Dee was deciding he didn't want to be a vegetable anymore. We thought that our love for one another was strong enough that we could overcome anything if we tried hard enough. Our relationship was like platinum: strong, precious, and timeless. We were basically two kids from Queens who fell in love and grew up together. We experienced the highest of highs and the lowest of lows, and through it all we were totally committed to each other and our marriage—but it was certainly a day-to-day struggle.

I knew Dee Dee had problems, but I believed that with love, hard work, a stable home life, and sobriety, the challenges that we faced could be overcome, and we could achieve our goals and make all our dreams come true. His past history was filled with drug abuse, sexual scandals, and bizarre behavior, but despite all of that, nothing would change my mind. We were very much in love, and as of

September 2, 1978, we were married, for better or worse.
Little did I know that I was in for the wildest rollercoaster
ride of my life.

A young Dee Dee Ramone.
From the Vera Ramone King collection

A teenaged Dee Dee Ramone.
From the Vera Ramone King collection

Dee Dee, Vera, and roadie Matt Lolya
hanging out in February of 1978 at the
Tropicana Motel in Santa Monica, CA.
From the Vera Ramone King collection

Dee Dee and Vera during a
visit to Disney World in 1978.
From the Vera Ramone King collection

The gang at Disney World. (L-R) Tommy Ramone, Monte A. Melnick,
Arturo Vega, and Vera Ramone.
From the Vera Ramone King collection

Dee Dee backstage.
From the Vera Ramone King collection

Dee Dee and Vera after their wedding.
From the Vera Ramone King collection

Dee Dee with President of Sire
Records, Seymour Stein.
From the Vera Ramone King collection

Dee Dee with his mom, Toni, in the garden after the wedding reception.

The bride with her parents, John and Rose Boldis, before the wedding.
From the Vera Ramone King collection

(L-R) Joey, best man Joel Tornebenne, Danny Fields, Dee Dee, Seymour Stein,
Arturo Vega, and Linda Stein.
From the Vera Ramone King collection

At the wedding reception at Villa Bianca in Queens. (L-R) Tommy, Seymour, Linda, Danny, Fernando, a friend of the Ramones, Joey and Susan Palmer, Monte A. Melnick, and Arturo.
From the Vera Ramone King collection

Mr. and Mrs. Dee Dee Ramone,
September 2, 1978.
From the Vera Ramone King collection

Sid Vicious, Dee Dee, and fans hanging
out backstage, London, 1977.
From the Vera Ramone King collection

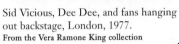

Vera reunited with Dee Dee in
London, after their wedding,
October, 1978.
From the Vera Ramone King collection

Monte (R) at a
European airport in
1978 with a Ramones'
roadie wearing the
"Pinhead" mask.
From the Vera Ramone King
collection

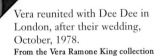

SUOMI FINLAND

Dear Vera
So nice to be
back in Helsinki.
Great to talk to you
on the phone. The
Finish people are very
nice to us and are
giving me the
Super Star Treatment.
See you in England
Love Bunny

Vera Colvin
21-07 157str
Whitestone NY
21 11357 USA

A postcard Dee Dee sent to Vera just days after their
wedding in September, 1978.
From the Vera Ramone King collection

The Ramones' friend Sid Vicious
on a Sex Pistols tour in the late
1970s.
Photo by Ron Ross

Celebrating Vera's birthday at the New York
hotspot Max's Kansas City, August, 1980.
From the Vera Ramone King collection

Dee Dee with friend and legendary Los Angeles DJ, Rodney Bingenheimer.
From the Vera Ramone King collection

Dee Dee with friend and fellow American rocker Eddie Van Halen.
From the Vera Ramone King collection

Tommy, Joey, and Dee Dee in Atlanta.
From the Vera Ramone King collection

Dee Dee in Germany, during the Ramones' 1979 European tour.
From the Vera Ramone King collection

Phil "Philthy Animal" Taylor from Motorhead with Dee Dee, backstage after a Ramones concert.
From the Vera Ramone King collection

Vera's view from backstage, Madrid, 1980.
From the Vera Ramone King collection

Dee Dee performing in Madrid, September, 1980.
From the Vera Ramone King collection

◄

Vera and Dee Dee at the gates of Graceland in 1978.
From the Vera Ramone King collection

Sightseeing in Europe with Arturo Vega.
From the Vera Ramone King collection

Dee Dee backstage after
a sound check in Austin,
Texas.
Photo by Lindell Tate

Dee Dee and Monte in Australia, 1980.
From the Vera Ramone King collection

Dee Dee with Japanese fans in July, 1980.
From the Vera Ramone King collection

Dee Dee and Vera's get-away retreat.
From the Vera Ramone King collection

Dee Dee, playing at Randy's Rodeo in San Antonio, Texas, in 1978.
Photo by Ron Ross

Max the Cat.
From the Vera Ramone King collection

Dee Dee with nephew T.J. Nienstedt,
playing guitars.
From the Vera Ramone King collection

A blonde Angela with Joey Ramone.
From the Vera Ramone King collection

"President Dee Dee" of the United States of the Ramones—given to Dee Dee by a fan.

Bob Gruen, renowned photographer and friend of Dee Dee and Vera Ramone.

The rock-and-roll couple at their favorite N.Y. spot: Max's Kansas City.

Dee Dee, Linda Stein, and British singer/producer Peter Asher at the Santa Monica Pier, 1978.

Dee Dee at the Armadillo World Headquarters; 1st tour, July 14, 1977.
Photos by Lindell Tate

Randy's Rodeo; 2nd tour, February 14, 1977.
Photos by Lindell Tate

Dee Dee at Randy's Rodeo; 3rd tour, 1977.
Photo by Lindell Tate

Randy's Rodeo. (L-R) Joey, Dee Dee, Johnny, and Tommy, 1977.
Photo by Lindell Tate

Mr. & Mrs. Dee Dee Ramone

It was time to fasten my seatbelt and hold on for dear life. Every day was a new adventure, filled with drama and unexpected turns. The Sunday morning after our wedding, Dee Dee had to leave for Helsinki, Finland, and we were both really depressed that we had to be separated so soon after the ceremony. Our honeymoon was going to have to wait until I could join him in London two weeks later, after which the tour would continue for another three weeks. Those two weeks seemed like an eternity to me.

Between facing sudden separation from his new wife and the anxiety of beginning the Ramones' European tour, it was all too much for Dee Dee. By the time he got to the airport to depart for Helsinki, he had medicated himself with a concoction of Tuinals, Quaaludes, Seconals, and Valium to the point where he could not even stand. That was bad enough, but then the flight was delayed two hours, and Dee Dee had to be physically carried onto the plane by the crew and Monte. Needless to say, this was not a good start for the tour.

Once he was in Europe, Dee Dee phoned me five or six times a day, or whenever he had a spare moment. (Dee Dee also sent me the most precious, romantic letters from tour, telling me how much he loved and missed me.) In those days, phone calls were expensive—there was no such thing as an unlimited calling plan—so our phone bills quickly added up to two and three times our rent in New York. It ended up being much cheaper for me to join Dee

Dee on the road, and the change was better for both of us. We hated being apart from each other, and he relied on me to keep him company, away from drugs and alcohol, and most of all, away from the groupies. Even though every member of the Ramones had his own fans and groupies, Dee Dee always attracted the most bizarre and fascinating weirdos and druggies. They just gravitated to him like a magnet, even in the most remote parts of the world. There was certainly no shortage of drugs or women trying to get close to him, ever—they always seemed to be crawling out of the woodwork. So Dee Dee never had to go looking for trouble...trouble found *him!*

It didn't take me long to realize that there were several duties and responsibilities I had to undertake besides simply being a good wife to Dee Dee. Even though I didn't work full time anymore, my job had become a 24/7 situation: taking care of Dee Dee Ramone and his very specific needs. He liked and expected things done in a certain and timely way—his way. After all, he *was* Dee Dee Ramone, rock star, so I just sort of accepted his unusual demands and learned to roll with the punches, sometimes literally. I tried to always be calm, cool and collected, and to get him to be less self-destructive. When he wrote the song "Time Bomb" it truly was autobiographical. Dee Dee came across as exactly that—a ticking time bomb—but I did my best to try and add some stability to his crazy life. In addition to being his wife, best friend, caretaker, bill payer, life organizer, personal hairdresser, babysitter, head to beat on, personal driver, and personal manager, I was also his rehabilitator. Just getting him sober was a job for ten men alone. My work was certainly cut out for me, but I wasn't deterred; I knew we were both committed to our relationship for the long haul. Nothing and no one was going to stop me from protecting my man, and I was going to do whatever I had to do to make sure we made our marriage work.

We were home only for a short time after the European tour when we were invited by Sid Vicious, bassist for punk band The Sex Pistols, and his girlfriend, Nancy Spungen, to hang out with them at the Chelsea Hotel. Sid, infamous in his own right, had always been infatuated with Dee Dee and idolized him for some time. I knew all too well what hanging out with Sid and Nancy meant and going to the Chelsea did not sound like a good idea to me at all. The last thing I needed was to get into a fucking fight with crazy, big-mouthed Nancy Spungen and have Dee Dee shoot up heroin with Sid. We politely declined the invite, only to find out a couple of days later that Nancy had been found stabbed to death the next day in their Chelsea Hotel room. We were back on the road when we heard the news; Dee Dee and I just looked at each other in complete shock. They apparently arrested Sid, and he was being held at Rikers Island on $50,000 bail. Dee Dee had been somewhat disappointed that we decided not to hang out with them at the Chelsea Hotel that night, but he didn't put up much of a fuss. He went along with my initial instinct and, after hearing what happened to Nancy, he knew that it had been the right thing to do.

We were still on the road a little while later when we heard about Sid also dying from an apparent overdose of heroin. The whole band was stunned and in shock when the news broke on the radio in the van. We all had phone calls that night from various people in New York who confirmed the sad, sad tragedy that the legendary Sid Vicious was dead as well. That night the Ramones even dedicated a song to Sid during their set to acknowledge the truly unfortunate loss of a special friend and fellow punk rocker.

Not long after Dee Dee, the band, and I returned home from our "honeymoon" in England, we headed to Los Angeles where the Ramones were set to film *Rock 'n' Roll High School*. This was a huge deal for the band. The opportunity to go to California and be in an actual movie directed by Allan Arkush and co-staring Clint Howard, Vince Van Patten, and P.J. Soles was very exciting for everyone. They were hoping that this would finally get them the airplay and recognition they deserved and worked so hard for. But despite the movie, interviews, record signings, and all the sold-out shows, the Ramones remained an underground band—their sound was just too radical for the airwaves. Only some college stations would dare play the Ramones.

The filming of *Rock 'n' Roll High School* marked two very important events for me personally: It was then that I experienced Dee Dee's first drug overdose, which happened at the Tropicana Motel on Santa Monica Boulevard in December of 1978, and when I first met and befriended Joey's girlfriend at the time, Linda. Linda and I quickly hit it off and became best friends. The four of us, Joey, Linda, Dee Dee, and I, actually had a lot of fun together on and off the road.

One night, Linda and I ventured to the corner grocery store and left the boys alone for barely twenty minutes at the Tropicana. When we came back, they were no longer to be found anywhere at the hotel. Soon we discovered that there was a party being held in one of the rooms on the other side of our bungalows. Tish and Snookie from the Sick Fucks, the Dictators, and the Dead Boys were having a party, and the place was overflowing with punks, all the way into the adjacent parking lot. And there, in the middle of the room, with chaos all around them, were Dee Dee and Joey having a jolly good time. By now, someone had given Dee Dee a handful of Quaaludes, Tuinals, and some methadone, and God only knows what else. He was drinking hard liquor and doing lines when I found him. But it was too late; the damage had already been done. Dee Dee was completely incoherent, running around like a lunatic in a state of frenzy.

Eventually the Los Angeles County Sheriffs were called because of all the commotion. They headed straight towards the loudest and baddest boy in the room, Dee Dee, who was anything but willing to be handcuffed and taken down to the station. The harder they tried, the worse he was, so they called for backup. At one point there were no less than four officers trying to restrain him, to no avail. Finally, he collapsed right there in the parking lot—he wasn't moving, wasn't breathing, wasn't doing anything at all. I stood there shaking, in tears, as they arrested Dee Dee and took him away in the ambulance. All I remember hearing was that it was called in as an overdose, and then they took him away and restrained him in handcuffs nevertheless. What a nightmare that night turned out to be! All I could think about was whether or not Dee Dee was going to survive. *Was he going to make it?*

I spent the rest of the night crying in my room, hoping he would be all right. Of course I didn't know then that this was only the first of many overdoses to come. In the morning Monte took me to Cedars-Sinai Hospital to pick Dee Dee up and take him back to our temporary home of three months, the Tropicana Motel. Seeing him in the hospital bed was such a relief. I was just glad he was alive. We hugged each other and cried and couldn't wait to leave the hospital together and put that awful experience behind us.

A couple of weeks after the horrific overdose incident it was Thanksgiving 1978, and we were invited to heiress Dana Magnum's house. Her family owned the Magnum department store chain, and Dana herself had just married a prince who bought her an island as a wedding gift. We had never heard of anything like this! She was good friends with Carolyn Zecca and her then-boyfriend, Joel Tornebenne, who'd been Dee Dee's best man at our wedding. We were excited to be going to such a high-profile socialite's party, especially considering all of the other rockers and celebrities that were invited. Dana's was a whole new world, for us anyway, and we eagerly went to see how the other half lived. Upon our arrival at her mansion in the Hollywood Hills, Dana was very gracious, and Joel and Carolyn introduced us as though we were rock royalty. Dee Dee *was* filming a movie and was about to start recording with the legendary Phil Spector, but being at Dana's was overwhelming for us. After all, we were just two kids in our mid-twenties from Queens, New York, and this was something so new and completely different than anything we had ever imagined.

I remember the place was filled with all sorts of celebrities. We were introduced to Jackson Browne, who had a huge album out at the time. I thought he was so nice and cute. He befriended Dee Dee right away, and they seemed to have a lot in common. We partied with him upstairs for a good portion of the night. Also at the party we met The Tubes, whose hit "Don't Touch Me There" was getting a lot of airplay. Two of the band's members, Re and Prairie, were married, and they remained good friends of ours for years.

Afterwards, we were all mingling downstairs, where the champagne was flowing and there were candy bowls full of white powder left and right. Everyone there was doing lines. It was while we were downstairs that Mick Jagger started hitting on me in full view of the whole party. I was very flattered. *Mick Jagger? Me? You've got to be kidding!* There were much better-looking women in the room. I figured he must have had too much to drink or something. Dee Dee and I stood there and ignored his comments, until Joel finally told him, "She's *married.*" His reply was, "Aren't we all!" He was still married to Bianca at the time, but there were rumors circulating about their supposed marital problems. Despite the awkwardness of the moment, Dee Dee was flattered, and he held on to me even tighter. I could tell it made him as proud as a peacock to be with me. All in all it was a great night, and a memory we both cherished.

Later that week, Marky Ramone brought Velvet, a black drug dealer famous to the many rockers who stayed at the Tropicana during those years, to our hotel room to smoke some marijuana. That would have been bad enough on its own, but after Dee Dee smoked with Velvet we found out that that the pot had been laced with angel dust. Oh, that was *just* what we needed! No sooner did they leave than, all of a sudden, Dee Dee began to freak out and proceeded to trash the hotel room as well as me. I called Dana, who was the only person in L.A. that I knew not associated with the band, and she sent her driver over to pick me up immediately. From there I flew to Joel's house in San Francisco where I recuperated for nearly a full week before I agreed to return to L.A. and put that horrible night behind me. I hoped that Dee Dee had really learned his lesson and that everything would be okay, but that was just wishful thinking on my part.

After filming *Rock 'n' Roll High School* the Ramones started recording the full-length album *End of the Century*, with legendary producer Phil Spector. We were all so excited, thinking that maybe Phil could finally make the music and sound of the Ramones more radio friendly. The band worked really hard to write songs that could be played on the radio, but only one DJ was playing the Ramones in Los Angeles and that was Rodney Bingenheimer, who was known for discovering some of the best bands of the '70s, all the way up through the '90s.

Rodney was a true fan of the Ramones and had a weekly radio show at KROQ where he played punk rock and other styles of music that were considered "cutting edge." Rodney's show specialized in all that was new and cool. The Ramones did a live interview with him on the air in which they talked about *Rock 'n' Roll High School* and what it was like working with Phil Spector in the studio. Rodney also asked Dee Dee point-blank if the rumor was true that he had gotten married recently. Johnny glared at Dee Dee, and he had to respond with "No, not true…it was just a rumor." Dee Dee was deathly afraid of pissing off Johnny and would never want to ruin the band's image. I remember standing in the next room and listening to this live on the air. It was hurtful to me at the time, but I knew why he had to deny our relationship. When they walked out after the interview, Johnny stared me down with a smirk on his face that said it all.

For the Ramones, recording with Phil Spector was a big deal. He was considered a master of sound and an interesting character, even at the end of the 1970s. Before the recording began, Phil invited all of the Ramones and their wives and girlfriends to his mansion in Alhambra, which was truly an honor. We all piled into the van, and Monte drove. As we pulled up to the huge gate and waited to be buzzed in, I noticed that the place looked more like a castle than a house. I don't think any of us had ever been in a place like that. After getting through the gate, there were two more electronically monitored doors with security cameras that we had to be buzzed through. We might as well have been going to see the President at the White House.

As we walked into the Spector castle, I remember seeing a huge winding staircase with lots and lots of pictures on the wall, all the way up to the ceiling. There were pictures of Phil with John Lennon and Yoko, the Ronettes and Ronnie Spector, the Shirelles, Ike and Tina Turner, Sonny and Cher, and so many other fabulous people that he had worked with over the years. It was very impressive. Phil never came to greet us at the entrance. Instead, as we entered the main living quarters, we saw and were greeted by Grandpa Munster himself, Al Lewis, sitting in a big chair with a high back. I remember Marky being the first one to shout out, "It's Grandpa!" Then we all hollered, "Grandpa!" and went over to introduce ourselves. Lewis was very friendly, but it was obvious he had been sitting there for quite a while, because he was pretty much intoxicated by the time we arrived. We waited with Lewis for at least an hour before Phil made his grand entrance and bestowed us with his presence. Soon after we were led into his private recording studio where he blasted all of his hits for us over and over again. He referred to his "Wall of Sound" and what his plans were for *End of the Century*, focusing especially on "Baby I Love You," which was going to be the first single from the album.

As Phil repetitiously played his songs over the course of the evening, Dee Dee became entranced watching Phil perched in his favorite chair, holding a big, gold, jewel-encrusted goblet. He looked like Count Dracula drinking blood out of a chalice. Finally Dee Dee couldn't contain himself any more. He blurted out to Phil,

"Let me have some of that." He must have thought he was missing out on something. So Phil turned to him, extending the goblet and said, "Ok, Dee Dee." Dee Dee immediately took a few large gulps only to realize it was Manischewitz wine. All the while Dee Dee thought it was some magical potion, but the joke was on him. Phil loved drinking his Manischewitz wine and would often go to the bathroom to drink it during the recording of *End Of The Century*. Almost everyone was wasted while recording that album, guaranteeing that there was a drama-filled fiasco nearly every night.

After listening attentively to Phil's albums, he decided we should all watch his new favorite movie, *Magic*, starring Anthony Hopkins. We watched as Phil rewound his favorite parts and showed the movie again and again, just like he did with the songs. By this time it was six o'clock in the morning, and Dee Dee and I were exhausted. Johnny had somehow managed to leave around midnight, but Dee Dee and I had to beg and plead with Phil to let us go home at 6 a.m. We couldn't just leave and walk out the door because we had to be electronically buzzed out; it was up to Phil to let us leave. Eventually he said that we could go, but he couldn't understand why on earth we wanted to leave so early. In a way, we had felt like we were being held hostage in his house. The whole evening was very weird, and it made Dee Dee uncomfortable being around eccentric Phil. More than anything, he had little patience for the producer's ultra-controlling idiosyncrasies.

Doing this record was going to be a real challenge, but was it going to be worth it? The studio by now had been booked, and each night—the band only recorded with Phil at night because he never came out of his house during the day—they'd show up and have to wait for Phil to arrive with his two bodyguards in tow. The waiting gave Dee Dee anxiety, and somehow he managed to take Tuinals and Seconals, whatever he could score, every night before the actual session, to help him cope. Phil had his own quirky way of working and would have the band, minus Joey who recorded his singing parts separately, perform their parts each night over and over and over again, maybe forty or fifty times, all night long. It was as if he had Obsessive-Compulsive Disorder or something. This eventually drove Dee Dee over the edge and after one long night, he just snapped. He threw his bass down on the ground and started walking out, saying, "Fuck this." As he approached the door, Phil motioned to his big bodyguards to stop him from leaving and pulled a gun on him. After this, the whole band was held hostage in the studio at gunpoint. Phil seemed to really enjoy the power that he had intimidating them with his gun, and it worked. After what seemed like hours, Phil finally let them leave, but it was a few days before they agreed to go back to the studio again and finish recording the album.

It certainly came as a relief when each of the band members got their parts down, and the album was finished. The band did numerous interviews, promotional events, and record signings for *End of the Century*, as well as starring on *Top of the Pops*, a very popular show in England. It was while the Ramones were shooting their *Top of the Pops* episode that we met and befriended Bryan Adams, who was also performing on the show. To our amazement he was a huge Ramones fan and was more intrigued with meeting Dee Dee Ramone than we could have imagined. He was even wearing a black leather, Ramones-type jacket with jeans, and the admiration between Dee Dee and Bryan was mutual.

Then the band performed on *Old Grey Whistle Test,* another popular show. Everyone, including me, had high expectations for the first single, "Baby I Love You," but the reviews were mixed, and the song got a mediocre response. True Ramones fans were expecting a different sound from the band, something more punk. In the end, they just couldn't please everyone. *End of the Century* didn't turn out to be what the Ramones, or their fans, had hoped for, and so they decided to return to their original roots for their next album.

After the recording and a slew of press events, we all returned home where the Ramones played in local venues. Finally, we could be in our own house and in our beds! Up until that point, we'd barely spent any time in our apartment at all.

It was that summer, in August of 1979, when Dee Dee decided he wanted to throw me a private birthday party at Max's Kansas City, where we first met. He contacted Laura and Tommy Dean, the owners, and the private room downstairs in the back was reserved. One hundred of our closest friends and family attended, and it certainly ended up being a memorable birthday for me— one that I'll cherish forever. Dee Dee rented us a white stretch limo for the night and had some surprise guests for me, including David Johansen and Syl Sylvain of the New York Dolls. Rock photographer Bob Gruen took pictures that were later featured in the centerfold of *Rock Scene* magazine.

CHAPTER SIX

The Whitestone Years

Living in Whitestone, Queens, was great in many ways. We got to spend time with our families and friends, and Dee Dee could finally start focusing on his sobriety. In 1980, he voluntarily joined a rehabilitation clinic called Odyssey House on 6th Street, between 1st and 2nd Avenues; Dee Dee was an outpatient at Odyssey House for many years. There he befriended a wonderful man named Harold Holloway, who became his personal counselor and, eventually, good friend. He was a really positive influence in Dee Dee's life and coached him through many years of difficult and turbulent times. Besides going to Odyssey House twice a week for counseling and supplying urine specimens that were mandatory as an outpatient, Dee Dee also saw a psychiatrist every week, Dr. Hann. He also started attending Alcholics Anonymous meetings on a daily basis, sometimes twice a day if he didn't have to play a show that night. It was during this time that he was diagnosed as being bipolar with manic depression, and he was given several anti-psychotic medications to take on a daily basis.

Between the Thorazine, Tofranil, Stelazine, BuSpar, Antabuse, and Valium, Dee Dee would smoke almost an ounce a day of the best weed money could buy. His dealer was on speed dial, but even his psychiatrists and drug counselors agreed that smoking pot was the least of his worries—not shooting up was a big step in his life! In the beginning, Dee Dee wasn't that into smoking weed, but he quickly replaced heroin with smoking major amounts of marijuana. His day would start with a huge joint and lots of coffee. We would wake 'n bake throughout the whole day. Like his doctors, I was just glad he wasn't shooting dope anymore.

Although Dee Dee took his sobriety very seriously, he was quick to substitute his dope habit with other addictions. He was very generous, sometimes to a fault. He loved to buy people presents and was extremely giving when he was in a good mood. On our tenth anniversary he surprised me with a gorgeous ring made of a twelve-carat, pear-shaped aquamarine stone surrounded by three carats of diamonds. Earlier we had seen it in the window of a local jewelry store as we were passing by, and I casually commented on how beautiful it was. Little did I know that Dee Dee went there and bought it for me.

The next day he insisted I go to the jewelry store to find out how much the ring actually cost. The jeweler was in on the plan and told me that it had been sold. I was so disappointed! When I returned home, I told Dee Dee that it was too late; the ring had already been sold. He tried to console me when he saw how disappointed I was. All of a sudden, he whipped out a small box and gave it to me with a great big kiss, telling me that he loved me more than life itself. To my amazement, it was the ring I wanted—it had been sold to him! I cried and cried with so much emotion and was completely overjoyed. Dee Dee was always that spontaneous. He loved to see the joy in people's faces and the happiness his generosity gave them. Over the years, I witnessed him giving many friends all kinds of gifts. In a way he was sort of like Elvis; he didn't have the kind of money that could buy people Cadillacs, but he had the same very giving heart.

It was during the spring of 1981 that we had enough money to buy a brand-new car: a light blue, metallic Camaro with a T-top. We were so proud of that car. We could finally get rid of our old, silver-and-maroon vinyl-topped Monte Carlo. Even though I was Dee Dee's official chauffeur, when we got the new car he assured me that he was a good driver and used to drive in the past. He told me about one time when he had to drive from Queens to Manhattan to meet the band for rehearsal. Dee Dee was driving over the 59th Street Bridge in a Volkswagen Beetle when it stalled and died right there on the bridge. He couldn't get the car to start or even move it to the side of the road, and he got really mad. He said he just got out and walked away, leaving the bug on the side of the bridge!

Even before I heard that story, I'd had serious doubts about his driving abilities, but I knew that neither one of us had ever had a brand-new car before—it wouldn't be fair to not let him drive his own car. As soon as he got behind the wheel for the first time in many years, it was apparent that he needed to brush up on his driving skills, and we both agreed that a few professional driving lessons would do the trick.

So, for the next month or so, Dee Dee had a driving-school instructor pick him up at the house for some personal one-on-one driving lessons. I was so happy that he was going to start driving himself everywhere, but this seemed too good to be true, and soon I was to experience what kind of driver he really was. He was an absolute maniac behind the wheel. Just like in real life, there were no rules that applied to Dee Dee, or to his driving. The only driving he was capable of was driving me crazy! If someone were to cut him off in a lane, he would step on the gas and tailgate the car while giving the finger to its driver. I tried to explain to him that this was New York, and if he wasn't careful, he was going to fuck with the wrong driver one day—someone who could just take out a gun and blow his head off at a stop sign. He knew deep down inside that this was true and that his road rage would eventually get him in hot water. (He had road rage before there was even terminology to describe it!)

One day, for some strange reason, Dee Dee told me that his driving instructor would no longer be coming over and assured me that I shouldn't worry. I thought this quite strange and sudden but didn't question him and resumed my role as designated driver. I continued driving Dee Dee around everywhere for years: to the psychiatrist in Manhattan every week, to the Odyssey House twice a week for counseling, and even just to piss in a cup two times a week if he had to play a gig. There was also driving him to all his AA meetings, NA (Narcotics Anonymous) meetings, and CA (Cocaine Anonymous) meetings on a daily basis—morning, noon, and night.

These regular meetings were all over Queens and Manhattan, and I would have to sit and wait outside in the car until they were over. Sometimes I would just drop Dee Dee off and pick him up one or two hours later. Then he'd want me to drive him to Forest Hills, so he could write songs with Mickey Leigh (Joey Ramone's brother), or to Manhattan, so he could write songs with Daniel Rey. Occasionally I'd have to drive him to Ira Herzog's office, who was his accountant, or to get tattoos. Many times I'd drop him off at Richie Ramone's house to write songs, or to the Plasmatics' Ritchie Stott's house.

That's what Dee Dee did best! He loved to write songs, all different kinds of songs, with different artists. Everyday he wrote something new. Writing songs and creating music came as naturally to him as brushing his teeth or breathing. Although he wasn't perceived as having a high I.Q., he was actually very bright. There wasn't much that would get past him.

Just like in any other relationship, with Dee Dee and me, there were always certain things that one of us was able to do better than the other. That's why Dee Dee left the driving to me, while he continued to do what he did best: write songs, and drive me and everyone else crazy. One morning as we were getting ready to leave to drive him to Manhattan for one of his many appointments, I noticed that a foot of snow had fallen overnight. I casually mentioned to him that we would have to shovel the snow off of the car before we left. Before I could get my boots and coat on, he was already outside, literally shoveling the snow off the car. As I approached the car, I looked at him, and we both noticed, at the same time, that he had actually scraped the paint off of the hood of our new car with the shovel! There they were: three to four big, long scrapes down to the bare metal. When I said that we should shovel the snow, I didn't think he would literally take the shovel to the paint. Oh, well, what was done was done! Dee Dee was Dee Dee, and I should have known better!

But for all of Dee Dee's wild antics, he had a very loving side to him. As I've said before, he had many different wonderful qualities about him, and he should be known for them as well as all the other things he'd done in his life.

I remember one bitter cold night in December 1983, four days after Christmas, when we returned home to our apartment in Whitestone at about 2:30 in the morning. The Ramones had just played New York City's

Ritz that night, which was owned by our good friend Neil Cohen. It was always a sold-out event when the Ramones played there. As we got ready to go to bed later that night after the show, we all of a sudden heard a lot of noise and footsteps pacing frantically over the hardwood floors directly above our bedroom. This was particularly strange because above us lived a lovely older couple in their 60s: Richard Salas and his wife of over forty years, Aida. Aida's widowed older sister Anna, who was in her 70s, also lived with them. They were very quiet people who went to bed early; if there was any noise coming from the Whitestone place, especially at that hour, it would have been from our apartment.

Upon hearing this commotion, I immediately looked at Dee Dee and shook his arm and said, "Listen. There's something wrong!" He heard the franticness as well and agreed that something was definitely not right! I put on my robe and he put on his pants, and we both went upstairs and knocked on the door.

Anna opened the door, hysterical, and pointed to the bedroom, speaking inaudibly. Aida was standing over Richard's side of the bed, and she was gasping for breath and just as white as a sheet. Immediately, Dee Dee ran over to Richard, and within seconds he had started giving him mouth-to-mouth resuscitation, pounding on his chest to keep his heart going while I called 911. Richard was having a major heart attack! Dee Dee tried his best to save him and wouldn't stop until the paramedics and ambulance arrived. They declared him D.O.A. as he was, sadly, already gone. But even though Dee Dee knew it was more than likely that Richard had stopped breathing, he refused to give up. I stood there in disbelief watching how quickly Dee Dee reacted. Aida was so grateful, saying it was very heroic of Dee Dee to have done something like that for a neighbor he hardly knew.

I was proud of Dee Dee and how he had really stepped up to the plate, and I called him "My hero." He was truly brave that night. Eventually we went back down to our apartment and held each other tight and cried over what had happened.

After Richard passed, Aida practically adopted us, and we gained in her a wonderful new friend. She was like our grandma and had keys to our house so she could check on it when we were away for long periods of time. She would keep an eye out for our place and for us. To this day, our first encounter with Aida and Richard is certainly one of the most amazing things that stand out in my mind when I think of the "other" Dee Dee—the Dee Dee that many people never saw or even knew existed.

What really drove Dee Dee crazy were Johnny Ramone's controlling ways. He was the self-appointed boss of the band and would override the opinion or point of view of anyone else. Nothing could be done without Johnny's approval or consent. Even though Johnny never wrote one single song, except for an occasional repetitious rift, he would critique and intimidate Joey and Dee Dee and their songwriting. And his controlling ways weren't just limited to songs. He would make rules for the whole band professionally and personally, and if you went against him in any way he would make life absolutely miserable for you and treat you like an outcast. Everyone feared the wrath of Johnny! He was nice to his fans, but he had a whole other side to him that we all experienced and were victims of at one time or another. Not only that, but the man could hold a grudge like no other. Don't get me wrong, we all had our own issues, and Dee Dee and I were no different. No one was perfect, and after we were on the road for long periods of time, sometimes three months at a clip, we would all get stretched pretty thin. Too much togetherness for anyone is a breeding ground for hostility and resentment. It was Johnny's controlling manner that earned him the name "The Fuehrer"—and rightfully so! We—being all the Ramones with their wives and subsequent girlfriends—were a part of his private boot camp. If you strayed from his rules you would pay a dear price, and he made sure of this. It didn't matter who you were.

Johnny also had a very low opinion of women—all women. He considered them inferior and insignificant and thought that they should be seen but not heard. Never in all those years did he acknowledge the opinions of any of the wives or girlfriends, until Linda came along. Linda was officially Joey's girlfriend. Johnny's girlfriend at the time was Roxy, a supposed heiress to the Vanderbilt-Whitney family in Chicago. He would keep her in the house most of the time because she had an alcohol problem and would cause him a lot of problems, not to mention embarrassment. Besides keeping her in the house, he beat her up on a regular basis to make sure she stayed in line. This is what led to the famous and well-known incident that was documented so famously on the front page of the *New York Post* in August 1983.

After a local gig one summer night, Johnny was dropped off at his apartment on 10th street that he shared with Roxy. As he approached the front door of his building, Johnny saw Roxy standing outside, totally drunk, with a guy called Johnny Angel whom she befriended after a wild night partying at CBGB's. Johnny was infuriated and made some kind of derogatory comment that swiftly led to Angel attacking him until he was down on the concrete. Angel's beating didn't end there. He repeatedly kicked Johnny in the head with his steel-toed, punk-rock combat boots as he lay on the concrete sidewalk. Johnny was subsequently taken to the hospital, fighting for dear life. That situation was the last thing Johnny wanted to happen. That's why he always kept Roxy at home: because she couldn't be trusted to go out without causing some kind of trouble. Of course, he enjoyed the control he had over her, and she weathered the abuse in return, actually taking it as a sign of Johnny's love for her. How sick was that? It was none of our business though—we had our own issues to deal with! I felt sorry for Roxy and empathized with her.

I remember Dee Dee and I were watching the eleven o'clock news the night after Johnny's attack when the newscaster suddenly said, 'Rock Star Fights For His Life—The story right after this commercial break." We sat there, thinking, "Wow. Who could that be?" When they returned to the program, a big picture of Johnny flashed across the screen, and they went into detail about what had happened the night before. *How come no one told us?* We quickly called Monte, who confirmed the story, although he had heard about it at the same time as us. In those days, Johnny hadn't had a telephone in his house for years. He used a payphone on the corner to make all his calls. It was during his hospital stay that Roxy saw Linda come to the hospital to visit Johnny and that really freaked her out. The truth about Johnny and Linda was finally coming to light, much to the chagrin and disbelief to all of us in the Ramones' small circle of players.

CHAPTER SEVEN

The Italian Bank Robbery

A few years before Johnny's head ever got kicked in, at the start of 1980, the Ramones, including Dee Dee and I, were headed back to England and Europe for a tour that was to last for the better part of six weeks. We proceeded to Amsterdam by ferry from London, where they played with the UK Subs at the Paradiso Club. Since smoking weed was legal there, Dee Dee gave me specific instructions to buy all the *hashish* that was for sale at the venue, while they were playing. The hash was supposed to last us the entire European tour—we were forbidden to bring any drugs from the United States through customs on our way to England.

I waited in line and ended up buying the pot and hash store out; after I left they closed it down. Everyone behind me in line hissed and yelled as I walked away from the hashish bazaar. They were only selling nickel and dime bags, and even though I was instructed to buy everything they had, all that amounted to was barely an ounce and that would hardly suffice. That wouldn't be nearly enough to get us through till the end of tour!

Each day of our European adventure we witnessed the friendship of John and Linda getting stronger and stronger. Even though Roxy was also with John on the road, and Linda was Joey's girlfriend, it was obvious to everyone that there was something going on between Johnny and Linda. John was not particularly friendly with Joey, but he and Linda were becoming chummier with every passing day. By the time we were in Belgium, they were coordinating their outfits! One morning, as everyone was piling into the smelly old bus to drive to Milan, Italy, we all noticed that Linda and John were wearing matching peach-colored sweatshirts. John never dressed like this before, and it was clear that Linda's sense of style was rubbing off on him. I could see the anguish in Joey's eyes; he was helpless against John. Linda was slowly succumbing to John's controlling ways, and there was nothing Joey or anybody else could do about it. Their private soap opera was unfolding in front of all our eyes.

There is an unwritten rule that any band member knows: You don't sleep with another band member's girlfriend or wife. Sure, there are groupies from time to time who get passed around from one to the other, but a wife, fiancée or steady girlfriend you do not sleep with. Never! That kind of behavior is what breaks up bands, and it almost broke up the Ramones. Needless to say, the tension in the air during the 1980 European tour was so thick that Dee Dee medicated himself to the extreme. He was well known for taking things—everything—to the extreme, but his drug abuse only contributed to the daily drama that we were all entwined in.

When we finally reached Milan, since it was still early after Dee Dee and I had checked into our hotel, we hurried to the bank down the block to exchange our American dollars for lire. I remember us walking in behind two guys, who got in line just ahead of us. Meanwhile, we waited in line for at least forty minutes. Other customers came and left, but we were still standing in the same spot. Dee Dee started to get real impatient and was showing his usual signs of being on the verge of a major breakdown.

What could possibly be taking so fucking long? There were only two or three people ahead of us! Finally we got to the window, exchanged our money, and proceeded to leave the bank so we could go somewhere and have dinner—we were starving by that point.

As we approached the door and stepped outside, we noticed that the whole bank was surrounded by Italian Policia cars, at least eight of them, and they all had their guns pointed at us. *What the fuck?!* They threw us up against a car with our hands held up behind our backs. Everyone was talking loud and screaming in Italian, and we had no clue what was going on and couldn't understand a word anyone was saying. In the crowd of people that had gathered around the scene I saw Monte and our tour bus driver walking down the block. I yelled to Monte, and he and the bus driver, who could understand a little bit of Italian, approached the police. They were told that we were being held because the police thought we were with the two guys who had been in front of us in line and that we were trying to rob the bank. The two dudes supposedly handed the bank teller a note to hand over the money—no wonder it was taking so long. The bank had notified the police, and the building was being surrounded as we waited inside. Monte and our driver explained to the police that we were with the Ramones, a punk band from America that would be playing a certain well-known local venue the following night, and that they had made a huge mistake. Dee and Dee and I were totally freaked out; we hadn't even been in town for fifteen minutes, and already there was a major problem.

After much speculation and conversation and what seemed like forever, they finally agreed to let us go. The whole incident was totally unbelievable and embarrassing.

By the time we were relased, there must have been a few hundred people gathered outside. I wondered, *How could this have happened?* I guess when we entered the bank we looked a little different than the average Joe there, but to think that we were with the bank robbers in front of us... what a nightmare!

Despite the chaos surrounding our first day in town, the Italian fans and shows were amazing. Italy is beautiful and full of history and romance. Aside from that one close call, we really enjoyed being there. I remember riding in the tour bus through the Italian Riviera on our day off before the Ramones played in San Remo. San Remo was incredibly beautiful and picturesque too.

After getting up early and having breakfast at our hotel one morning, Dee Dee and I decided to do some sightseeing, and we walked hand in hand through the gorgeous little village. It was so scenic, like something out of a Grace Kelly and Cary Grant movie. The sky was vivid blue with puffy white clouds, and the water looked so gorgeous with the sunlight bouncing off the top of the waves like a trillion dancing diamonds. We walked down the narrow cobblestone streets and ventured into the many wonderful shops along the way. The vendors were all very friendly to us, their American customers, and when we finally reached the marina, we sat down to have some cappuccinos. We were surrounded by expensive yachts and looked up at a narrow road, winding up to the top of a cliff, which overlooked the magnificent city of San Remo.

Dee and I both felt like we were tripping, engulfed by the sheer beauty of this magical place. More than anything else, it felt so good to be together and away from the rest of the band and all the tension and animosity we were all going through. This tour was especially difficult to endure, because we were subjected to the cruel and unfathomable reality that was slowly unraveling in front of our eyes as Johnny pursued Linda, much to Joey's utter despair and total humiliation.

After several hours frolicking about San Remo, Dee and I headed back to our hotel. It was siesta time, and all the shops in town were closed from about 2 to 5 p.m. So we decided to go downstairs and hang out by the fabulous pool for some R&R and to catch some rays. After a couple hours of ultimate relaxation, we returned back to our room and made love like it was the first time. The day had been perfect—I didn't want it to end. Dee Dee was so wonderful: attentive and sweet, like a knight in shining armor who would protect me at a moment's notice and fight for his woman if he needed to. He was always very protective of me like that. I know he enjoyed this special time we had together as much as I did, and we vowed to one day return here for a second honeymoon, the real honeymoon that we never had.

After the Ramones' Italian dates, we headed to Madrid, Spain. Spain was also breathtaking, and we had a lot of fun there as well. In Madrid, the Ramones were scheduled to perform on a Spanish TV pop show. Well, as Dee Dee and I approached the steps of the TV station, who did we see but Eddie Van Halen himself. "Hey, Eddie, fancy meeting you here!" There was instant camaraderie meeting another American rock star so far from home. To our great surprise, Van Halen was making an appearance on the same show as the Ramones.

At the studio, each member of the Ramones was given his own dressing room, and it wasn't long before Dee Dee had disappeared with David Lee Roth to smoke a few spliffs somewhere. Eddie had come to hang out with me in our dressing room. He had just recently wed Valerie Bertinelli, and we exchanged stories about being on the road and missing our respective spouses while touring the world. It's hard enough to keep a marriage together when things are on a somewhat normal schedule, but the rock and roll lifestyle makes it twice as hard, and almost humanly impossible when there is substance abuse, alcohol, and groupies to contend with. The rock lifestyle is quite a challenge, and I give a thumbs-up to all of the rock and roll couples that have stayed together despite the many pitfalls and obstacles that stood before them. Some couples, like Tina Weymouth and Chris Frantz, Sting and Trudie, Sharon and Ozzy Osbourne, Alice Cooper and his longtime spouse, Dee Snider and wife Suzette, and even Slash from Guns N' Roses and his wife Perla have made it work—families, tour buses, temptations, and all. I admire and respect the couples who have made it work in this business and have overcome all the obstacles that come with this lifestyle.

CHAPTER EIGHT

Gabba Gabba Hey!

In July of 1980, after the Ramones' European tour, we were headed for Japan. Going to Japan was especially exciting for the band, since the fans there were real fanatics. Every show sold out, and afterwards the fans, all dressed up like adorable mini-Dee Dees, wanted to pose for pictures with their favorite Ramone. I remember that they were so respectful, and it was customary for them to give you a little gift, such as a comb or something they'd made especially for you. They were very nice and kind people.

We were in Tokyo playing at a sold-out venue with Sheena and the Rokkets, who were opening for the Ramones. I remember looking out into the audience from the side of the stage. The music was so loud that night that the balconies were physically swaying from side to side. I thought to myself, *Boy, they're really rocking the house tonight!* Backstage, after the show, the band was told that they had actually played through an earthquake. But they never missed a beat and the show went on.

Afterwards Dee Dee invited some fans back to the hotel room to smoke and drink *sake.* Even though I liked smoking weed, I never really drank. On rare occasions, I would have a sweet, girly drink, but I definitely didn't drink beer. I tried the sake, but it didn't appeal to my taste, so I stuck to my diet soda. Dee Dee, however, liked the sake, perhaps a little too much. After everyone had left the room, he got ready to take his ritual evening bath in the deep, really short tub the hotel provided. Soon enough, I learned just how much pot and sake Dee Dee had had, because he was too intoxicated to get out of the tub. I desperately tried pulling him out, but to no avail. Help! I thought he was going to drown himself in the tub. I quickly called room service and asked them to send someone up to please help stop Dee Dee from sinking right in front of me. Two hotel employees drained the tub, and the three of us tried to get Dee Dee up and out of there. Somehow after about fifteen minutes—maybe more like twenty—we finally got him onto the bed. Ironically, the next morning he was up early and didn't remember a thing from the night before. He actually commented on how refreshed he felt and what a good night's sleep he'd had. I was glad *someone* had a good night's sleep.

After touring Japan, the band's next stop was the beautiful and welcoming country of Australia. During our "off" day, we went to the zoo, where we got to hold baby koala bears, and Dee Dee was chased by an ostrich. He had tried to feed it, but the ostrich started chasing him instead. It was hysterical. Monte wouldn't even let him go near the kangaroos, for fear he would somehow manage to get punched out, and it would affect the tour. Monte had a tough time dealing with this bizarre bunch, each member with his own set of strange quirks. He certainly had his hands full and then some.

The next stop on the tour was New Zealand. By the time we got there, the temperature was zero degrees. I remember being so very cold that I decided to stay at the hotel and skip hanging out in the ice-cold dressing room. But the warm hotel room turned out to be anything but warm. The hotel room was so cold that I called the concierge and asked for, not one, but two portable heaters, and even then the room didn't warm up. We had stayed in at least one hundred hotel rooms since the Ramones started touring, but this one was especially, oddly frigid. My only consolation was that soon Dee Dee would be back from the show, and we could cuddle to keep each other warm. He finally came back to our room after the show and had in his shoulder bag a pair of wet jeans and a wet T-shirt (that he had worn during the show), and some wine, which he had apparently started drinking on his way back to the hotel. When he came into the room, he also noticed how cold it was and continued drinking, although not to the point of being totally drunk. We were lying on the bed, watching television, when all of a sudden he began to speak in some strange language.

At first I thought he was just joking, and I laughed at him. He wasn't laughing back; instead, he started speaking in foreign tongues, in a weird voice! Even though I've never seen him or anyone else speak in "tongues" before or since, it reminded me of a scene straight out of the *Excorcist*. I started getting really upset and shaking him, screaming, "Stop it! You're scaring me." But he continued as though he hadn't even heard me. It was as though some kind of entity had entered his body and was taking over him. *What the fuck?* I was scared shitless. During that whole episode, I was totally freaking out, unable to snap him out of that state. Finally, as quickly as it had started, it stopped. Dee Dee resumed his own personality. When I explained to him what had just happened, he only vaguely understood what I was talking about. He knew that something had taken over him but was clueless as to what it was. We both got scared and were more than relieved to be leaving the hotel the next morning. I know I didn't sleep a wink.

I will never forget what happened that night in Christ Church, New Zealand, because whatever it was, however unexplainable and weird, it was real. People can say Dee Dee was crazy but that had nothing to do with his possession; I witnessed it firsthand. Something took over him for a short period of time, of this I am sure. And once you've experienced something like that, you don't ever forget it.

Finally, we were on our way home, and that day couldn't have come too soon for me. The thirty-three-hour flight home, after being on three continents, was about all we could handle. I remember, in the airport at the end of the tour, Marian (Marky Ramone's wife) was pushing Marky around in a wheelchair so he would get preferential treatment boarding and leaving the plane. The whole band plus their wives and girlfriends just stood there in amazement, watching and wondering how in the world he managed that scenario. Marian was wheeling Marky around like he was a disabled person! We found it absolutely hilarious, and in a way, I think Dee Dee was jealous that he didn't come up with the idea first.

We had barely gotten home from "down under"— I now know why they call it that—and Dee Dee had barely put down his bags, when he announced he was going to Manhattan to get his regular supply of magazines, usually about thirty to forty dollars worth. What he failed to mention was that he was also going to get his well-deserved fix of heroin, which he had been planning the whole way home as a reward to himself for finishing the last stretch of the tour. Arturo had given each band member his share of the T-shirt money at the airport, and Dee Dee certainly couldn't wait to go downtown for some Chinese Rock. He came home a few hours later with a huge bag of assorted magazines, cigarettes, pot, and more.

What was the end of a grueling schedule for everyone else was just the beginning of new drama waiting to unfold for me. It seemed like I never got a break. *What about some down time for me?* Well, I got my wish! My down time came in the form of a 102-degree temperature and the flu. So while I was in bed half dead, Dee Dee was in the living room, high as a kite and surrounded with all of his favorite things: knives, magazines, pot, cigarettes, and whatever else he liked. I could have lain there dead for two days before he would have noticed anything was wrong. When I finally emerged from my bed, after a day or so, I noticed a trail of small, white, little pills across the room that had fallen out of a hole in the pocket of Dee Dee's jeans. I questioned him as to what they were, and he denied that they were even his and said he had no knowledge of where they'd come from. I was too weak to continue the conversation so I made myself a cup of tea, took some antibiotics, and went back to bed.

I woke up a few hours later to a house filled with thick black smoke and no Dee Dee. He had gone out to get more drugs while I was sleeping and had left the glass coffee pot on the stove where it burned, turned black, and filled the house with smoke, nearly burning the house down in the process. I opened all the windows and doors and had to stand outside to get fresh air. Thankfully, the landlord was at work and didn't come home to find that one of his tenants had almost burned down the house. You can only imagine the conversation that took place when he got home later that evening.

With Dee Dee, I was constantly asking myself, "What's next?" My job was 24/7 and the truth is, there was never any down time for me. Even as Dee Dee slept, I would keep one eye open to make sure he was still breathing and had not overdosed. It was not unusual for him to swallow a handful of Thorazines and literally be crawling over the bare floor on his hands and knees. It was sad to watch this and hurtful to witness the downward spiral of such a wonderful and multi-talented individual as he succumbed to his totally drug-induced escapades, which were slowly winning over his struggle with addiction. I felt hopeless and scared and had never experienced anything quite like this. *What do I do? Who do I turn to? Who could I trust with the daily horror I was living?* In many ways, living with Dee Dee was like living with an A.D.D.-inflicted five-year-old—or like living in an Iraqi war zone. Now that I think of it, what the hell was I thinking? I never knew what was next, but I totally believed with my whole heart and soul that together Dee Dee and I could beat this battle and that, one day, life together would be wonderful and easy. Towards the end of us, however, I realized that I was buying into a fairytale that was never going to come true.

We had a two-week break before the Ramones were scheduled to play a show in Long Beach, Long Island. I was actually looking forward to Dee Dee playing. It meant that he would have to be straightened out by then so he could face the band and perform in the show and not be fucked up. Being in the band gave him a sense of discipline and responsibility, and he knew that his drug behavior would not be tolerated—not on their time and not on their dime!

But during Dee Dee's time off he did things besides drugs; he developed other addictions. He'd go to his accountant's office and harass Ira for money, or he'd go to see his manager, Gary Kurfirst, and make a pain-in-the-ass of himself on a regular basis. He also wrote new songs, sometimes based on the last tour's experiences, and he would go to his AA meetings and attend his other programs. All in all, there was never a dull moment and definitely never a boring day. There was something going on every waking minute. We had lots of fun together too. We would do things like go see a movie the first day it was out, when no one else was there. I remember going to Manhattan, on Third Avenue somewhere, to see *Elephant Man*, which had just been released in a limited number of theaters. One of our favorite things to do was to go shopping on 8th Street and St. Mark's Place. I loved buying boots, and Dee Dee loved buying sunglasses— prescription only, of course. We loved to shop at Trash and Vaudeville. The help there was always so nice to us. Natasha had her own boutique right across the street and would make me custom clothes, cool outfits that no one else had. Trash and Vaudeville would also customize my clothes, like when they studded the bra cups on my black spandex minidress or customized a jacket for Dee Dee.

He and I also went to quite a few premieres, parties, openings of exciting new clubs, and to see new bands play at the Ritz, a venue that was owned by our good friend Neil Cohen. Going backstage when performers like the Clash, Adam and The Ants, or Madonna were playing was always a lot of fun. We often frequented CBGB's on Saturday afternoons to see the new punk groups like the Suicidal Tendencies and the Circle Jerks, just to name two. Then we would go for Mexican food on Third Avenue or to our favorite Indian restaurant on 6th Street. When Dee Dee was sober, he would often wake up in the morning and decide exactly what he wanted to reward himself with that day. Most of the time he bought jewelry or got tattoos on Long Island somewhere, or he'd buy a new watch. He had this *thing* for watches, and while I had nothing against him collecting watches like his switchblades, it was when he wore seven of them at the same time that I had concerns.

Dee Dee was the same way with his tattoos—almost obsessive. When he had to fly to L.A. to film the video for "Psychotherapy," he rewarded himself for his sobriety with a big leopard on his upper left arm. Everything he did had to be recognized with a present to himself, which was fine with me, as long as he wasn't being self-destructive. He also wrote daily journals, recommended by his therapist, to express his feelings and emotions on paper instead of acting them out. These writing exercises helped somewhat, but Dee Dee would get bored easily, and when that happened, trouble usually followed.

When he wasn't getting tattoos, he was buying diamond hearts at Fortunoff's on Fifth Avenue for me or his mother or anyone, really. He enjoyed making people happy because he wanted to make up for all the pain he caused when he was mean and fucked up. Nevertheless, I loved Dee Dee unconditionally, whether he was poor, sick, rich, or mean. I loved him for better or worse, and we would have stayed together if he had stayed on his meds. Without them he was too volatile, and I was scared for my life, afraid of becoming just another statistic.

After we broke up, and he quit the Ramones four weeks later, Dee Dee became more and more bitter and irrational. Each week he became more drugged out and got more out of control with every passing year. At the end, everyone was his enemy.

CHAPTER NINE

A Complicated Man

Once the band and Dee Dee and I were back in the states, we were in our car one day, waiting for the light to change on Francis Lewis Blvd., when Dee Dee noticed a young homeless man who sort of resembled Joey. This guy was tall, lanky, barefooted, and wearing jeans with holes in them. His hair was long, dirty, and scraggly looking. He stood on the corner, repeatedly tapping his shoeless foot from the sidewalk to the street. The image must have looked all too familiar to Dee Dee because as the light changed, Dee Dee yelled to me, "Move over! Move over!" I pulled the Camaro to the right and parked by the bus stop. Dee Dee jumped out of the car, ran up to the homeless kid, and just handed him a twenty-dollar bill. "Here man. This is for you," he said. As Dee Dee walked back to the car, the young man looked at the bill and yelled to Dee Dee, "Are you crazy?"

But I remember several other instances where Dee Dee gave his money to homeless people. When we would be in Manhattan, waiting to go through the Midtown Tunnel, there was always an abundance of homeless people happy to wipe our windows while we waited for the light to change. And Dee Dee always gave them money. To this day, I can hear him saying to me, "That could've been me." He never thought twice about giving strangers what little he had.

One Christmas I bought him a black cashmere, three-quarter-length coat from Bloomingdales. It was expensive and gorgeous. Two weeks later, one freezing-cold January day, Dee Dee came home after being in the city. He was ice cold when he came through the front door. I asked him, "What happened to your coat?" He just said he had given it to some guy down on the Bowery. "What?" I yelled. "You gave that nine-hundred-dollar coat away?" He said he felt sorry for the guy—he was living in a cardboard box. This was the Dee Dee I knew and loved. He had always had a big heart, and this time he literally gave a guy the shirt off of his back. Few people knew that Dee Dee had many different sides to him. Those people can only recall seeing him stoned or totally fucked up, but the truth is that he had many touching and loving qualities about him. Still, secretly, deep down in my heart, I had suspected that there was more to the coat story than Dee Dee was telling me. I'd had a hunch that he traded his beautiful black coat for some kind of drugs, but I gave him the benefit of the doubt and never said otherwise.

A bizarre example of Dee Dee's generosity having disastrous effects happened when Stiv Bators from The Dead Boys was at our place one day. He was admiring a switchblade of Dee Dee's. The knife was one of his favorites, but Dee Dee thought nothing of giving it to Stiv on the spot as a present. Stiv was elated and showed it to Sid Vicious, who went to 42nd Street to get a knife exactly like it. The one Sid bought was the blade that was eventually used to kill Nancy Spungen.

I learned very early on that Dee Dee had a fascination with all kinds of knives and switchblades. As we traveled around the world, his hobby was buying and collecting switchblades from every country where the Ramones played. He also ordered them from various mercenary magazines, like *Soldier of Fortune*. They were illegal in this country—this much I knew—and were probably illegal to transport to various other countries too. Dee Dee would just give his knives to the roadies, so they could be hidden amongst the sound and lighting equipment, which was the only way they could be smuggled into another country without being confiscated by customs.

After many years of collecting, there was a time that his private collection of knives had accumulated to about two hundred, maybe more. Once in a while he would give one away to a friend or fan who admired it. Like with the homeless, Dee Dee was very generous in that way; if you told him you liked something, he would give it you. I didn't mind so much that he had such a vast collection of dangerous weapons, but what really concerned me was when he would be high and would sit on the floor for hours in his room, surrounded by all of his weapons and entertaining himself by flicking blade after blade repeatedly. Watching him do this was extremely alarming—I was deathly afraid that he might accidentally injure or stab himself.

In addition to his large blade collection, Dee Dee had also acquired several sets of nunchucks, the martial arts weapon comprised of two wooden sticks connected to each other by a small chain, which could be dangerous— or even fatal—if handled improperly. He would whip them around the house, intimidating everyone around. Continuing his obsession with deadly instruments, Dee Dee had a large collection of mercenary and "How to Kill" books and magazines that featured weapons used primarily for fighting and killing. He also joined a karate class that he would go to twice a week when he was home for a while. We attended several World Wrestling Federation (WWF) matches at Madison Square Garden in New York and always watched wrestling on TV when we were home. He and I were both huge fans. We even had the pleasure of meeting the wrestlers Superfly Snuka and Sergeant Slaughter, as well as Captain Lou Albano, and Cindy Lauper, who was a frequent guest on the WWF program.

Although he was fascinated with these weapons of death, I never witnessed him killing anything. But the whole idea behind the weapons—the world of danger and fighting that they represented—occasionally came through in some of his song lyrics. Dee Dee was an extremist in every sense of the word. It was always all or nothing, and he truly lived the phrase "Sex, drugs, and rock and roll"—maybe not in that order, but definitely so!

Dee Dee was a binger. He would be sober for a while, and then something inside of him would snap and he'd go wild. If there was any cocaine around, you could bet that he'd find it or find someone who had it. He was a human dustbuster; lines the length of a coffee table were no challenge for him during his coke binges. I've never seen another human being consume such a vast variety of chemicals at one time. He would intoxicate himself to the point where, when he did finally pass out, I would sleep with one eye open all night just to make sure he was still breathing. What I soon learned was that there was nothing that anyone, including myself, could do for Dee Dee when these binges occurred. I felt helpless and was overwhelmed with worry. Luckily Monte was just a phone call away, and I depended on him and his help. He was more than the Ramones' tour manager—he was the glue that kept the band together. He did an excellent job, and I never thought they paid him enough for all the abuse he endured over the years.

Besides myself and Monte, the rest of the band and crew had also grown accustomed to Dee Dee's drug binges, legendary tantrums, and self-destructive behavior. Everyone involved with the Ramones was instructed to never get drugs for him. However, nothing would deter Dee Dee. It was as if he had radar; he could always find a way to accommodate his drug needs. He was less prone to getting into trouble when I was around, but even that didn't always stand in his way. Dee Dee was the king of lies and deceit. If I did go to a gig with him, I was on "drug alert" after the show. If I didn't go to a gig with him, I would be worried about what kind of shape he would come home in. Even I needed a break every once in a while, although rarely did I get one.

In addition to the drugs, there was a never-ending supply of local groupies. The groupies and drugs sort of went hand in hand, and still do behind the scenes in rock and roll—certain things will never change. Even though I was continuously helping Dee Dee during his struggle with sobriety, the one thing I did expect, no matter how bad things got, was monogamy. And he did manage to be faithful at least ninety-nine percent of the time. Between the AIDS epidemic being in full bloom and growing each year and my having already been infected with hepatitis and near death in our first year together, monogamy was my number one rule for Dee Dee; his sleeping around would absolutely not be tolerated. I knew of Dee Dee's reputation before we got together—everyone (men or women, it didn't matter) claims to have slept with him at one time or another—but I disregarded his past and tried to focus on our future together.

Still, it was never easy, and to make things even more difficult, the girls would actually find out our address in Whitestone, Queens, and set up camp on our landlord's lawn. They would come to the house and ring the doorbell early in the morning, sometimes in groups of five or more. I thought it was crazy! One of the main reasons we ever moved to Queens was so that we could have privacy and some sort of normalcy in our lives. Just going down the street to the local grocery store, across from the schoolyard, became an ordeal. Sometimes we would drive to the Korean section of nearby Flushing to purchase a pack of cigarettes. But no matter how annoyed he would get, Dee Dee wouldn't dare show his fans. He would graciously pose for pictures and sign autographs for them. He realized that without his fans, where would he be?

* * *

Every day with Dee Dee was another soap opera, another drama. He was originally diagnosed as manic depressive and bipolar; I had no idea what each day would be like and would be cautious to even speak in the morning when he got up. You never knew which Dee Dee you were getting! I would be afraid to say anything because even the littlest thing could set him off and make him snap. I walked on eggshells every morning until he decided the mood of the day and who would be his victim. As long as I wasn't on that list everything was fine. But if I *was*, things got ugly really fast. Coffee cups would be flung across the room fifteen minutes after he got up.

This was especially true if John had said something to him after the show the night before, or if he'd received an early morning phone call from his manager's office at Overland Productions, or Andrea Starr, or Ira Lippy. Any one of those people could send him into a tailspin. Unfortunately for me, I was the sounding board and very often the victim of his out-of-control rages. Most of the time I would try to pacify him and calm him down by being the voice of reason, but I had to be careful with what I did and didn't say. Just one wrong word would make me his enemy too.

Dee Dee was always feeling like the victim, thinking everyone was somehow secretly conspiring against him. He acted paranoid, especially when the Ramones were getting ready to put out a new album. Since he and Joey wrote all the songs, Dee Dee felt the pressure to create and deliver. The weight of putting out a new album and writing songs that pleased Johnny fell heavily on Dee Dee. But Dee Dee created some of his best work under pressure.

His usual routine when preparing for a new album would be getting up, writing lyrics, and composing a song each day. At rehearsal he would present it to John, who would critique it, sometimes telling him that it wasn't good enough, or it wasn't "Ramones appropriate." John's comments would drive Dee Dee over the edge and make him feel crazy, because no matter how good the song was, being critiqued by someone who never wrote any songs or lyrics was hard for him to take.

Often Dee Dee would be so irate that he would physically force Monte to drive him to 10th Street after rehearsal, so he could cop some drugs before he was taken home. Monte would try to refuse, but many times Dee Dee would downright threaten him, reminding him whom he worked for. Sometimes Dee Dee would go to Arturo's where he'd be told there were no drugs, although that wouldn't deter him from getting what he wanted. After all, he was Dee Dee Ramone and Dee Dee Ramone got what he wanted, so fuck everyone! Arturo's house was party central and was pretty much deemed off limits for Dee Dee, but he always made such a pain-in-the-ass out of himself that they just gave him what he wanted to get rid of him. He even wrote a song on one of his solo Dee Dee King albums called, "I Want What I Want When I Want It." Oh yeah, that was Dee Dee!

I often blamed Arturo or the roadies for supplying Dee Dee with drugs, but it wasn't their fault, and I regret blaming the crew. Dee Dee had a serious addiction; if they didn't get drugs for him, he would have gotten them somewhere else. He was determined to get what he wanted, at any price, and he succeeded ninety-nine percent of the time. Although he attended his meetings on a regular basis, saw his psychiatrist every week, and took his medication, he would sit there and tell lies to the doctors, wasting their time and our money. Though Dee Dee died of an overdose at the age of forty-nine, one can only imagine what he was like in his twenties and thirties. Saying that he was a handful does not even begin to describe it! I often wonder how on earth I put up with such extreme behavior on a daily basis, but the answer is crystal clear: I really loved Dee Dee, and even though he was crazy at times, he definitely loved me too. After one of his episodes, with me as the victim, he was always so remorseful and tried to do everything he could to take back the pain he caused—but the damage was already done. Even three-dozen roses couldn't take away the physical and mental bruises that I suffered through.

One time in the early '80s we had a vicious fight, which ended in physical abuse. I fled for my life and went to my parents' house, where I stayed for several days, healing my bruises and giving Dee Dee time to calm down and come to his senses. While I was there, he phoned and begged me to come home, but I explained that there were certain conditions he would have to agree to before I'd step foot into that house again. During our phone conversation I could definitely tell that Dee Dee was under the influence of something. All of a sudden, in mid-conversation, he passed out. I kept screaming, "Dee Dee! Dee Dee!" and when there was no response from him, I knew something terrible had happened. I hung up the phone, dialed 911, and requested an ambulance be sent to our address right away. I explained that there was a probable overdose and they'd have to let themselves in; I was on my way and would meet them there.

Luckily, a family friend named Steve, who lived next door to my parents and was also a cop, happened to be home. I explained the situation to him, and he drove me to Whitestone in his undercover police car, the big red light flashing, at a speed that felt like one hundred miles an hour. We made it there in less than ten minutes. When we arrived, the paramedics were already working on him in a frenzy. The mere sight of Dee Dee, lying on the carpet with all sorts of tubes in him, and the police, who had just arrived, was overwhelming. I remember going completely numb from the anguish of hearing the paramedics say that they thought he was gone. By then, my best friend, Regina, and her sister, Renata, were by my side, along with other family members who had arrived to console me. I was so sick to my stomach that I felt like throwing up. If Dee Dee didn't make it, I wanted to die too.

I was just totally overcome with grief thinking, *If only I had been there, this never would have happened!* But what was done was done. Between my tears and pleading with the medics to save Dee Dee's life, I noticed that the police were looking around the house, and thinking quickly, I closed the door to Dee Dee's room, where he kept his pot and switchblade collection. One of the officers did pick up a switchblade or two and asked me about them. I told him that they had been gifts from fans. It was then that the paramedics said they'd done all they could—Dee Dee would have to go to the hospital. They asked me what kinds of drugs he could have taken because he wasn't responding to any of their antidotes.

I finally told them the truth: It could have been heroin, Tuinal, Quaaludes, maybe even Valium or cocaine…. I just didn't know! They put him into the ambulance, and Steve and I followed in the police car behind them. By this time, it seemed like the whole neighborhood was outside, looking to see what had happened and who was lying on the stretcher. (Actually, ambulances and police cars weren't out of the ordinary in front of our house; they were there more often than one would like.) On the way to the hospital, the medics were finally able to get a pulse and revive Dee Dee. I broke down into tears and was filled with relief, joy, anger, and disbelief all at the same time. The next morning I was able to take him home, after living through yet another one of his dramatic near-death episodes.

As usual, we were afraid to tell the band what had happened, but I could sense that they were beginning to feel just like I did—"What's next?" We all knew that you could cheat death just so many times, until one day when you weren't so lucky. Dee Dee was always so remorseful and apologetic after these episodes and promised to change his ways. He'd try, and it would work for a brief while, but then something would tick him off and he would snap. After that, it would be back to rehab for Dee Dee, like walking through a revolving door.

To temporarily help relieve stress, besides smoking pot, Dee Dee would take baths, sometimes as many as five or more a day. Every chance he got, he would be running a bath and then soaking away his woes. It had been a daily ritual for Dee Dee ever since I first met him. He would just lay there and soak and splash, and then the bathroom floor would be soaked with water and wet towels. Dee Dee certainly was the cleanest individual I knew, not necessarily the neatest but definitely the cleanest. I don't mean to imply that he wasn't neat. He was, in fact, very tidy and liked his surroundings kept at a certain standard that he had become accustomed to. Home-cooked meals, fresh linens and towels, and a clean house were must-haves for Dee Dee. Anything messy would make him uncomfortable and highly irritable, which no one wanted.

CHAPTER TEN

My Main Man

After having lived with Dee Dee for so many years, it became apparent that maturing with age was not on his agenda. Near the time of our divorce I was approaching thirty-eight years old, almost forty, and I realized that I needed someone with whom I could share the responsibilities as well as the joys in life. Dee Dee never wanted to grow up. Even when he was forty, he was still behaving like an irresponsible teenager. His temper tantrums were legendary. Nothing was ever his fault, and to be forty years old and blaming your problems on your childhood was getting real old. Knowing both his parents well, I realized that Dee Dee's upbringing wasn't any worse than the average person's; his childhood was a scapegoat, an excuse for refusing to grow up and into a mature and responsible man. Basically, Dee Dee was a man-child, a perpetual Peter Pan, and his way of dealing with life's problems was not dealing with them at all. Instead, his escape during tough times was taking drugs— self-medication was his answer to everything.

Aging is a natural part of life and not a choice that we are given. After all, who wouldn't want to stay young forever? But this is not reality for me, Dee Dee, or anyone else. Life is full of peaks and valleys, highs and lows, the good, the bad, the ugly, and everything in between. It is a journey full of experiences, and we are here to learn from them. That's where the old saying comes from: "wisdom comes with age." Wouldn't it be wonderful to know everything at the age of twenty that we know at the age of eighty? But that's not how it goes. That would be too easy! We're supposed to struggle and figure things out and learn through our many experiences. This difference in perspective became one of several obstacles that undoubtedly led to my split with Dee Dee. Unfortunately, some people don't, or won't, grow up, and there are few things worse than being a childish old man, or woman for that matter.

A good example of Dee Dee's immaturity came about one weekend sometime before 1985, when Dee Dee and I had agreed to drive my mother and sister upstate to the several-hundred-acre compound that my family owned. The trip was three-plus hours one way, and we still had to pick them up in Queens. Of course, Dee Dee was late coming from rehearsal as usual, and he knew we had a long drive ahead of us. To my complete and utter disappointment he showed up not only late, but also stoned on dope, with a beer in his hand. Dee Dee was ready and raring to go—and I knew that meant trouble.

We had barely made it out of Queens—we were on the New York State Thruway heading upstate—when he announced he had to pee, "Now!" What was I supposed to do? There were no rest stops, but I managed to pull over to the side of the road. There was a deep embankment, and because he was so stoned, Dee Dee could barely make it down the slope. After a few minutes of waiting, my sister and mother patiently sitting in the backseat of the car, it became obvious that Dee Dee could not make it back up the hill; he kept falling backwards and sideways. I had to get out of the car and physically push him up the embankment, and even then, he barely made it back to the car. My mother and sister didn't say a word, but I can only imagine what they thought. Dee Dee was clearly fucked up.

It became even more obvious a few minutes later when he had to relieve himself again. But this time, instead of having me pull over to the side of the road, he just whipped out his dick and pissed into an empty beer bottle that had been in the front of the car. I prayed that my family didn't see this from the backseat. Then, just before we reached the house, the beer bottle fell over and *rolled* to the back of the car, right onto my mother and sister's feet. They asked, "What's all this yellow liquid?" My quick thinking told them that it was the beer that had spilled out from the bottle.

As we pulled into the driveway, I cleaned up the mess as fast as I could. I never knew if they really believed it was beer or not, but I was still humiliated. I lashed out at Dee Dee, yelling, "How could you?" But he was so out of it, I don't think he even comprehended what I was saying. I can't—or don't want to—remember all the horrible things that resulted from Dee Dee's drug problems. I've blocked so much out, due to the embarrassment, pain, and humiliation that I suffered over the years, but there are still certain events—like that drive—that I wouldn't be able to forget if I tried. Needless to say, that was the first and last time I volunteered to chauffeur anyone from my family up north again. Once was enough.

After that weekend, I came home one afternoon to find Dee Dee in the spare room, which we called Dee Dee's Room. It was where he kept all of his records, books, clothes, weapons, and magazines. Dee Dee was sitting there, guitar-in-hand, in the middle of the room, on the newly installed carpet, with a huge circle of red spray paint around him. Upon deciding to paint his guitar (which I still own) red, he had gone out to the boulevard hardware store, while I was out, and purchased several cans of bright scarlet paint. There in his room, without any drop cloths, or newspapers, or anything else to protect the carpet, he had spray-painted his guitar bright red. I couldn't believe *what* I was looking at. Obviously he looked like he was as high as a kite, and I assumed he'd made his decision on impulse, just like everything else he did. Looking at the red paint on the carpet, all Dee Dee could say was, "Oops." We tried to clean up the mess, but it was hopeless; the carpet would have to be replaced…again. There was no point in fighting about it—that would have led to something even worse. No, this was just another ordinary day living with Dee Dee!

That weekend the Ramones were due to play in Asbury Park, New Jersey, as they had many times before, so Dee Dee had to be sober when he saw the band for the show. Afterwards, we were graced by the presence of The Boss himself, Bruce Springsteen, whose *Born to Run* album was high on the charts. Springsteen lived nearby at the time, and since he was not playing that particular weekend, he decided to stop by and see the Ramones play. He even came backstage and told the band how much he enjoyed the show. The admiration was mutual, to say the least. Joey asked The Boss to write a song for the Ramones, as he had done for Patti Smith. Bruce thought it was a great idea, but because of his and the Ramones' hectic schedules, it never materialized. The band felt honored that The Boss found time to come to the show that night, and they talked about it in the van all the way home.

After that show, it was back to business as usual for Dee Dee. One late afternoon, Dee Dee came home from the city with an eight ball of cocaine. I don't know how he had obtained it; his doctors insisted that he only carry a certain amount of cash on him, so he wouldn't be tempted to go out and cop drugs. He probably went to the bank, where they knew us personally, and took the money out. However he got the cash, I'm sure that it was part of Dee Dee's agenda for the day, along with an originally-planned visit to see his manager, Gary Kurfirst. So he brought home the coke, and we started to party.

By 1:00 a.m. I'd had enough, and ventured off to my room for some peace and quiet, although I soon realized that was not going to happen. Dee Dee started calling everyone and anyone in our phonebook who would have a conversation with him in the middle of the night. He just kept talking, hours and hours of nonsense. I tossed and turned in my bed, listening to him babble and carry on in the other room. Dee Dee even called his psychologist at 4:00 a.m. to have an in-depth conversation about how straight and drug-free he was going to be. What a bunch of crap! I don't think the man had a clue that Dee Dee was stoned on coke and talking out of his ass about his sobriety.

By about 7:00 a.m. he had talked to just about everyone we knew from New York to California. He had run out of people to harass but was still craving attention. I hadn't been able to sleep all night—all I wanted to do was crash—but Dee Dee finally came into the bedroom, and I had to fake being asleep. I just hoped that he would leave me alone—please! But that would have been too good to be true. He still wanted an audience and needed attention, anyone's attention, so he started up with the same old shit, ranting and raving and taunting me. When I refused to respond to his demands, he did what he would often do in the middle of the night: He took the lamp off of the nightstand in the bedroom and smashed it on the floor, stomping it into bits and pieces. He had done this not once or twice but maybe a dozen times. Well, he finally got my attention! I hated always going to the same store, at least once a month, to buy new lamps to replace the broken ones. The owners must have thought I had a lamp fetish or something—no one could need that many lamps.

On this particular morning, it was the last straw. I darted out of bed and ran into the kitchen to grab the biggest twelve-inch butcher knife I could find. I was in no mood to put up with Dee Dee's bullshit; he just wouldn't stop. I decided there and then that I was going to give him a taste of his own medicine. As I held the huge knife in my hand, I purposely displayed a look of sheer insanity on my face, like a woman driven to the edge. I glared at him and screamed, "What'd you say to me motherfucker? What'd you say? Repeat it again. I didn't hear you. Come on, big boy, you wanted my attention? Well, you got it!"

Then I started chasing him around from room to room. I *must* have scared him straight, because he immediately backed off and sat on the couch as quiet as a little mouse. Dee Dee had never seen this side of me and didn't know what to make of it. But I persisted and wasn't about to let him off the hook so easily. I wanted him to know exactly how it felt to have the shoe on the other foot and be afraid in the hands of a complete maniac. He needed to know how it felt to be on the receiving end of his lunacy.

"Oh, you have nothing to say now?" I asked him. "I thought you wanted my utmost attention. Go ahead, say what you said before. I dare you…. 'You want to be the next Nancy Spungen?' Don't fuck with me mother-fucker. Who's got the power now, big shot? You wanna know where I got this from? I learned it from you! How do you like it?"

His attitude and demeanor had completely changed. He sat there on the couch like a fucking altar boy. I knew exactly what I was doing, and I would never hurt anyone, but Dee Dee needed to know how he often made me feel threatened and fear for my life and safety. So, my reverse psychology had worked. I was Dee Dee and he was Vera— "How do you like it now?"

When I finally saw him humbled and remorseful, I put the knife back in the drawer. We got dressed, cleaned up the mess in the bedroom, and I made him come with me to replace the lamps for the umpteenth time. And I told him that from then on, he was gonna have to replace the lamps and keep paying for new ones—I was done. To my amazement, he never broke the lamps again, and that had gone on for literally years. So my plan worked. Dee Dee got the message loud and clear. I was so good at my acting that morning that I should have won an Oscar for my performance! What I learned from that experience was: When dealing with someone acting crazy, the only way to get them to stop is to act even crazier than them. They can't deal with that. Although I would never advise using this type of reverse psychology on a regular basis, because eventually something bad will happen, once was all it took to resolve the lamp situation. It worked like a charm, and Dee Dee never pulled that lamp stunt again!

CHAPTER ELEVEN

Our Getaway Retreat

It was in the spring of 1982 when Dee Dee and I invested some money we saved to enter a real estate partnership and bought an apartment building in Bensonhurst, Brooklyn. A friend of the family that I knew had owned several buildings in New York and Brooklyn, and she told me that if I found the right building she would teach me the ropes. We knew that if we found the right piece of real estate at the right price, it could be very profitable for us, and we made this our side project.

After searching and physically going and doing our homework, we found a perfect corner building in a nice part of town for a great price. We were so excited! I already had my hands full with Dee Dee, but this property would be my way of contributing financially. I could do this from home and work on my own time and still be there for him. This real estate venture was a lot of work and consumed much of my time. Sometimes Dee Dee came with me, but most of the time I dealt with the tenants, contractors, and any problems that arose, all on my own.

After three and a half years, all my hard work had paid off, and we sold it for three times what we had bought it for. There were three partners, and after the balance of the initial mortgage, closing costs, lawyer's fees, and taxes, the three-way split was still more than Dee Dee had made in the previous five years combined. We bought a gorgeous ten-acre estate as a retreat for ourselves in the Catskills. It had high ceilings, lots of glass, and a winding staircase and fireplace. This was to be our private getaway when Dee Dee would come home between tours. Our estate was very secluded with absolutely breathtaking mountain views. We loved going there because it was so quiet and serene, and Dee Dee loved shooting off his guns and doing target practice up there. That place was a great escape for him. We were away from the band and the city, and we tried to spend as much free time there as possible, even if only for two days at a time. Dee Dee was just a different person up in the Catskills.

Our neighbor on the other side of the property had a farm with cows, chickens, pigs, and some horses. I noticed on more than one occasion that Dee Dee would talk to the animals as though he was actually communicating with them. I think he loved animals so much because they didn't judge him or care who he was. He frequently could be seen out there having a conversation with his animal friends.

During one of our summer weekends upstate I noticed that he was in a foul, rotten mood from the minute he woke up. He took his guns and ammo and went to the area where he would do his target practice. Within a very short time he returned to the house and demanded that we drive back to the city—immediately! It was a three-hour drive each way, and we had just gotten up there. I told him, "Let's go tomorrow," but he insisted and started to fly into a rage, continuing his rant about leaving, "Right now!" He had gone from Jekyll to Hyde right in front of my eyes. How dare I question his request to leave at that very moment? The more I tried to reason with him, the more irrational he became. I should have known the price I was about to pay for being disobedient.

It had just started pouring rain, but Dee Dee wouldn't wait another hour. The next thing I knew, I had a gun pointed to my head, and I couldn't pack our shit up fast enough. I knew that if I didn't leave with him at that very moment, I might never be going anywhere again. I was sure he would have killed me. As we approached the New York State Thruway the gun was pointed at me from the passenger's side, and it stayed that way the whole ride back. With tears rolling down my face, I could barely see the road ahead of me, but I continued to drive. All the way back, he was saying the most horrible things to me and insisted that instead of going home, we go straight to the East Village, to Avenue B.

Suddenly I realized what was really going on. He wanted drugs—what else? I told him that I was driving over the George Washington Bridge to the Cross Bronx Expressway to Whitestone and that if he wanted drugs, he would have to take himself there. I'm not sure how I got the nerve to say that, but I *did*, and we finally got home. The minute he got out of the car he called a car service to take him to Manhattan. As soon as he left I grabbed a few things and left for my sister's house in Bayside. I didn't want to be home when he got back. I had just gone through four hours of pure hell and was lucky to be alive!

After he returned home, he called around looking for me. When I returned his call, he was angry—at me. Can you imagine that? I told him that he had gone over the line this time, and I needed some time to think about where this relationship was going. A couple of days later I found out that the gun he held on me was only a BB gun, and it wasn't even loaded. Intimidation gave Dee Dee a sense of empowerment, and he loved to be in total control. I should have known better, but I was scared to death: Anything was possible with him!

One night during a long, strenuous week, while the Ramones were preparing to work on their new album *Too Tough To Die*, Dee Dee got up in the middle of the night and locked himself in the bathroom with several switchblades. He claimed he was so depressed and just wanted to end it all. I stood at the other side of the door for several hours and pleaded with him to come out. Life was good; nothing could be so bad that he should want to cut it short. Dee Dee had a life most people could only dream of having. His future was bright. I told him how much he was loved, and how he would disappoint all his fans if he did something like this. He would let down so many people that looked up to him. But nothing I said could get him to come out of the bathroom. He just kept saying he was done and wanted to end it.

Out of sheer desperation I called my father at 4:00 a.m. and asked if he could help me get Dee Dee out of the bathroom and stop the suicide threats. I needed help! My father and brother were at our place in ten minutes. Dee Dee didn't look up to many people, but he very much admired my father and liked my bother John a lot. If he'd listen to anyone, it would be them. My father could see that I was desperate to have called him at 4:00 a.m.—he *knew* this was an emergency. Both he and my mother loved Dee Dee like he was their *own* son. My father talked to him through the door and spoke to him as though he was his own dad, father to son.

Finally, after about ten minutes, he came out crying like a little boy, and he hugged my dad and they both cried. Dee Dee thanked him and my brother for coming over at that hour of the morning. He needed to hear a father's voice and to know that he was loved, and that's exactly what my dad had said to him. He knew exactly how to handle him. Dee Dee had not had a close relationship with his own father for many years, but after we married, I tried to rekindle their relationship and eventually, after several years of estrangement, they became friends. By then his father lived in Atlanta, Georgia, and was not able to come to his son's rescue. After things calmed down, my dad and John left to go back home.

Thank you, God! I remember holding Dee Dee tight that night and assuring him that everything was going to be okay. The worst was over, and tomorrow was another day; it was a new beginning, and we were going to fight his demons together. I let him know that I was there for him all the way and that he wasn't alone anymore. His life was my life, and it was *our* life now. Everything was going to be all right. I promised him.

Joel Tornebenne called us one day after Dee Dee's suicide attempt. He was in New York and staying at the Stanhope Hotel on Fifth Avenue overlooking Central Park. He invited us to come spend the day with him. We didn't see him often because he lived out of town. For a while he lived in L.A., and later he moved to Woodstock, New York, where he lived near his best friend, Todd Rundgren. Whenever Joel came to town we would always go visit him. On this summer day, midweek, we had lunch with him at the Stanhope and later took a walk through Central Park. Then we went back to the hotel because Joel had an appointment and didn't want to be late. We were waiting in his fancy suite when he received a phone call. He excused himself and said he would be back in a few minutes.

About twenty minutes had passed, when he returned holding a huge piece of luggage with a big, bulky handle. The minute he walked in the door I didn't even have to ask what was in the suitcase—I could smell it! He placed the suitcase on the floor and unzipped it. There must have been at least fifty kilos of cocaine neatly packed in tight, clean plastic bags. I had never seen anything like this in my life, not then or since. *Wow! So, that was his appointment! That's why he was in New York! That's why Dee Dee and I were invited to the hotel!* I finally understood what was going on. Once Dee Dee saw Joel's package, his eyes lit up like a Christmas tree in the middle of July. It was hopeless to even try to drag him out of there. He would have sooner sent me home in a cab then leave now.

Joel proceeded to take out a bag. It was huge and tightly compressed. The smell was overwhelming even before the bag was opened. Then he put out finger-wide lines along the full length of the coffee table. Dee Dee "the Hoover vacuum cleaner" couldn't get down there fast enough with his hundred-dollar bill rolled up to snort the stuff. I also took a small toot, as I didn't want to be the party pooper. The shit was so pure it made me gag. But not Dee Dee! He couldn't believe his good luck. We had no idea what we were in for when we ventured to see our dear friend that day. I wouldn't have believed it if I didn't see it with my own eyes. It was something right out of *Scarface!*

Rock Wife

In 1986 the book *Rock Wives* by Victoria Balfour came out, and I was among several wives of prominent rock stars featured in it. She had contacted Overland Productions and requested an interview with me for her book on the wives and girlfriends of rock stars. I was truly honored to be included, along with the "significant others" of Brian Wilson, Jim Morrison, Keith Richards, Meat Loaf, Frank Zappa, Bob Dylan, and David Bowie to name a few. Victoria Balfour worked for *People* magazine at the time, and *Rock Wives* was her first book, as well as the first book ever written about "rock wives" at that time.

Dee Dee was very proud of me and encouraged me to participate in promoting the book when I was asked. Among others we did *The Today Show, Good Morning America, Live with Regis and Kathy Lee*, and *CNN*. I actually turned down two requests by Howard Stern; I was so afraid of any embarrassing questions that might come up because Dee Dee was in rehab again during this time, and I had to attend daily family therapy sessions. Plus, I was just plain scared! It was a lot of fun meeting some of the other wives who were a part of the book, and I made friends that I still keep in touch with to this day. Marilyn Wilson Rutherford, former wife of Brian Wilson of the Beach Boys, has remained a great friend over the years. We would always see her and the girls, Carnie and Wendy, whenever we were in Los Angeles and spent great times at their house and going out to eat. They in return would be invited as guests to the Ramones' L.A. shows and would always come backstage afterwards.

After our small book promotion tour, Vicky and I were invited by Leslie (Meat Loaf's wife) to come and spend the day up at their Westport, Connecticut, home. She and Meat Loaf had a lovely house that they shared with their two beautiful little girls, Pearl and Amanda. We had a wonderful picnic at the beach that day and developed a close friendship. A few months later Meat Loaf was booked to play the Palladium on 14th Street in New York City, and he and Leslie invited us down to the show to be their special guests. We went there with Richie Ramone and his wife, Annette Stark. It was incredible! Meat Loaf is such an amazing performer and never leaves his audience disappointed. Later we went backstage and hung out and posed for some photos. It was a real fun night.

For *Rock Wives'* debut, there was going to be a big party at the club Area, and Dee Dee had promised me he would be on his best behavior. This was a special night for me, and I didn't want him to fuck it up. Just to ensure his good intentions, he invited Harold Holloway, his counselor from Odyssey House, to be our guest, along with Barry Apfell and Jeff Kugler, his friends and AA buddies. This was so I would not worry about Dee Dee being up to any funny stuff.

Well, we arrived in our limo, and the place was packed! I wasn't sure how many people, if anyone at all, would show up. The guests included Joey Ramone and his girlfriend, Angela Galetta, Richie Ramone and his wife, Annette Stark, Matt Lolya and his wife, Laura, Arturo Vega, Janet Grubb, Monte Melnick, and Sire Records' President, Seymour Stein, who even brought Mo Austin's

(President of Warner Brothers) two kids to meet me. That night was so much fun, although I couldn't help but notice Dee Dee disappearing all night long. Every time I turned around from having a conversation with someone, he was gone. *Where was he?*

By now Harold had left, and it was getting late. Out of the corner of my eye I saw Dee Dee follow some girl to the men's bathroom and into one of the stalls. I followed him into the men's room and peaked through the crack of the door, where he was snorting coke up his nose like a human vacuum cleaner. I pounded frantically on the stall door, screaming, "I know you're in there!" The girl started saying, "It's not what you think...." She assumed I thought she was giving him oral sex, but I still wasn't about to cut her any slack. Then they opened the door, and I could not control my adrenalin from going through the roof. I physically pulled Dee Dee by the earlobe out of the bathroom as everyone looked on in awe, and we got in the limo and left. This was so embarassing, and it was a real problem. Who did he think he was kidding?

There was just no end to Dee Dee's constant need for finding someone, anyone, who would provide him with free drugs. It didn't matter where we were, or who we were with! It was as though he had radar for drugs and could always find something to get high on, even in the most remote places and backwards towns—in any city of any country. It didn't matter if he couldn't speak the language; he still somehow managed to find trouble. Needless to say, he ruined the book party, and all the "I'm-Sorrys" couldn't change that. He would be sober for a while again afterwards, but even though he really tried, he just couldn't help himself. Dee Dee was a binger, and when he went on a binge, it was always god-awful. One can only imagine the horror and abuse that I endured during these terrible times, and what he put everyone through!

The band witnessed firsthand the physical abuse that I was subject to. There was one incident that occurred in Dallas, Texas, after we left a 7-11 store where we had stopped for snacks. As we got back in the van, for no reason at all, Dee Dee started beating me, pulling chunks of hair from my head, punching me in the face until he had me on the floor of the van, and stomping on my head with his steel-tipped punk boots. *What did I do? Was it my fault that they were out of his brand of cigarettes?* Everyone just watched, and no one came to my rescue.

Finally Monte said, "Someone stop him before he kills her," to which Johnny responded, "Stay out of it! This is a domestic dispute." *A domestic dispute?* Dee Dee could have murdered me in front of nine people, and everyone was afraid to say one word. After fifteen or twenty minutes Monte had seen enough and put a stop to the abuse before I was killed in front of all of them. Thank God for Monte, or I might have died that night.

The next morning as I took a shower, chunks of hair were still falling out of my head and into the shower drain. My eyes and face were so swollen I couldn't see. It hurt to even put sunglasses on my face before I took a cab to the airport and got on a flight back to New York. Even as I sat on the plane the stewardesses looked at me and asked if they could get me some medical help.

Somehow, I made it back to New York. My head and face were swollen, as well as black and blue. My entire body was bruised like I had been in a tragic car crash. I did not dare go to a doctor because I knew they would have Dee Dee arrested for assault and attempted murder. I couldn't even get out of bed for at least a full week. I called my sister Sonja and made her promise not to tell anyone that I was home. She freaked out and cried when she first saw me. I was unrecognizable, even to my own family! She came over daily and tried to get me to eat something and help me get out of bed. This certainly was not the glamorous life of a rock star's wife that I had envisioned for myself. This was hell on earth. There was a big price to pay being Mrs. Dee Dee Ramone.

I just laid in bed and cried at the mere thought of what had happened. I struggled with staying in the relationship. Was all this worth it? Dee Dee called me at least five times a day, apologizing and begging me to forgive him. Despite all of our troubles, I was still so very much in love with him that I wondered who was crazier: me or him? Eventually, after a few weeks, he persuaded me to meet him in Florida and rejoin him on tour. Even after I flew there, I hid out at the hotel. I was still swollen and had two black eyes. I remember being on the balcony of the hotel looking down at the pool when Johnny walked out to the balcony in the adjoining room. He took one look at me and shook his head with sympathy when he saw my black eyes and bruised face. Johnny never showed any sympathy for anyone, but the sight of me made even him sick to his stomach. It was a horror scene that all of them witnessed, and no one ever forgot.

For all of our troubles, I do have to say that Dee Dee and I had the most wonderful, absolutely awesome Christmases together. Christmas was a special time of year for us, and we enjoyed it with my family. His mom, and even his grandmother from Germany, would come to my mother's house Christmas Eve and Christmas Day. We always exchanged our presents on Christmas Eve, and there was always an abundance of gifts, sometimes stacked four-feet high in the room. You could barely walk through the front door of the living room at my mom's because the presents were piled up so high. There were presents for everyone, and Dee Dee *loved* presents.

One Christmas in particular always comes to mind—the year when we decided to buy my sister, Ellen, a kitten. We went to the pet store on Northern Boulevard in Flushing where there were a number of really cute kittens. We picked several of them up and saw that each kitty definitely had his or her own personality. As we put them back down, there was one black-and-white one that just clung to me. No matter how hard we tried, we just couldn't get her off of me! She dug her little paws into my sweater and wouldn't let go. She was black and had white under her neck and belly and all white paws, and she looked just like she was wearing a tuxedo. Then they told us *she* was a *he*, but it didn't matter: This kitty wasn't letting go. He was coming home with us no matter what!

As it was a couple of days before Christmas, we had to keep him at our house until we could bring him to Mom's on Christmas Eve so that it would be a surprise. The next day I still had several errands to run to finish up my last-minute Christmas shopping, so I had to leave my "Max" alone with Dee Dee in the house for a few hours. He promised he would take especially good care of Max the Cat and told me not to worry. I mean, what could go wrong? Well, when I left him, he was sitting on the floor writing a song and holding Max on his lap.

After I finished doing my shopping and came home, he was *still* sitting there petting the kitty with a big joint in his hand. But I immediately noticed that something was wrong. As I leaned forward to take a better look, I was shocked to see that Dee Dee had singed all the cat's whiskers and eyebrows with the joint while he was petting him with one hand and writing a song with the other. Cats need these whiskers and eyebrows to keep their balance and determine the perception of widths and heights. They are their antennae, so to speak. I freaked when I saw its burnt whiskers and eyebrows. "How could you?" I asked Dee Dee. "What were you thinking?" He didn't even realize what he had been doing, but he felt so bad. How could he do this?

I couldn't give my sister the cat looking like this, so I took a pair of scissors and tried to even out each side of the whiskers and eyebrows as well as I could. I hoped that they would eventually grow back, and the cat would survive the trauma. When Christmas Eve came, we put a beautiful, little bright-red bow around its neck and brought him to my mom's house in a box. We kept him in the bedroom there until it was time to open all the gifts after dinner. Dee Dee was always anxious to get dinner over with so he could open the presents—that was all he cared about.

I always went out of my way to make sure I gave him the coolest stuff from Trash and Vaudeville in N.Y.C., and this year I had gone especially overboard, getting him several big, thick rap chains and a couple of huge gold rings from a jeweler in Flushing, Queens, who specialized in the new rap-jewelry frenzy that was catching on and becoming real hip. I got him the whole deal except for the gold grill, and all of it was real gold. I figured if he wanted the grill, he would have to get it made himself because they'd need to make a mold of his teeth, and then it wouldn't be a surprise! Dee Dee was like Peter Pan—his doctors actually said that he had "Peter Pan Syndrome," as everyone was getting older and more mature and responsible, he continued refusing to grow up. He wanted to be young forever in his mind, and this was a big part of his personality—and a big part of our eventual breakup.

We gave Max the Cat to Ellen, and she was totally overjoyed, but as the cat grew it was evident that the trauma had affected his neurotic-ness; he was never the same again! Despite that, the cat had a great home and unconditional love. But whenever we went to Ellen's house, and Max saw Dee Dee, he ran and hid under the bed. Oh well, we tried. Dee Dee was really trying to be affectionate; he never meant to hurt Max in any way and was very sorry. He was *always* sorry *after* the fact. But what was done was done.

During the Christmas holiday we were invited to many parties and club openings. At one of these events I remember we all got to meet and hang out with David Bowie, who was and still is a rock icon. We were with Danny Fields, Linda Stein, and Joey Ramone at the Mudd Club on this particular night and we had a blast! A couple of weeks later we went to the opening of a new club in Manhattan where we were introduced to Ozzy Osbourne. Ozzy had this necklace around his neck that had "#1" encrusted in diamonds. It must have been three inches in length. He told Dee Dee that it symbolized his one year of sobriety. In actuality it was probably one week or one month but who cared anyway? It sounded good, and if Ozzy could stay sober we figured there was hope for Dee Dee too! They exchanged several stories about their struggles with staying sober and attending AA meetings and got each other's phone number. We also hung out with Jean Bouvier and "Miami" Steve Van Zandt and his wife. He played with Bruce Springsteen and is now famous for his role in the popular cable show, *The Sopranos*, which is still watched by many.

* * *

The last Christmas Dee Dee and I spent together before our breakup in December of 1988, he gave me one of my favorite gifts that he had ever bought for me: a stunning and very fashionable faux-leopard coat. One day, a while later, we were walking down 8th Street in New York City by Patricia Field's store. He had his arm around me, as he often did, when we stopped to look at something in a punk boutique window. After nearly twelve years together Dee Dee and I still held hands everywhere we went, or he would keep his arm around me as we walked down the block. This was one of qualities that I loved about him. He always wanted me to feel protected and never hesitated to display his affection for me in public. That was just part of his demeanor and became a very natural way for us to walk around together.

After we stopped at the store window that day, we proceeded walking to El Quijote, one of our favorite Mexican restaurants, when I smelled something funny. I asked Dee Dee if he smelled it too. He replied, "Yeah! What is that?" To our horror, he had burnt a hole on the shoulder of my coat with his cigarette while he had his arm around me. "Oh, my God!" I said. "Look what you did!" I was absolutely freaked out. "How could you?" I asked. Of course he was sorry, but these kinds of things had become a daily occurrence by that point, and there wasn't much we could do to fix it. The coat was ruined, and it was just another ordinary day for us in a not-so-ordinary life.

CHAPTER THIRTEEN

Too Many Addictions

It was after the New Year, and the band had a little time off. Dee Dee got bored easily and was always trying to reinvent himself. I was his hairdresser and would dye his hair jet-black with Nice 'n Easy then cut it spiky and stick it up with Dippity Doo. When he wore his hair un-spiked, it was flat and quite short. It was during his time off that I noticed that he shaved his whole face as usual, except for a small patch that started under his nose and went to the top of his upper lip. In a week he had a Hitler mustache, resembling the very picture of the crazy, despicable German dictator. Dee Dee also started wearing a swastika-emblazoned Nazi armband on his upper left arm. I thought, *You can't possibly walk around looking like this. Someone will kill you!*

His new style was an insult to many people and a disgrace. But he purposely adopted the whole look and enjoyed the expressions of the shocked people he came in contact with. This time, Dee Dee had finally crossed the line: Both of his psychiatrists were Jewish, and even they couldn't figure out why anyone would adopt such a distinct look. And Dee Dee spoke fluent German to boot! He was a dead-ringer for the Nazi dictator, and when he wore his signature swastika I'd call him, saying, "Hey, Adolf, dinner's ready!" I was hoping and praying that this was just a phase and that he would shave off his offensive mustache and look like my *old* Dee Dee again. But I realized that the more people asked him to shave it off, the more determined he was to keep it. He loved being able to get a reaction from people and shocking the crap out of everyone. Dee Dee truly enjoyed causing controversy. So, I just decided to ignore it, hoping that he would just wake up one day and get rid of it on his own.

After a while he shaved it off, but now it was tattoo time. Every morning, for weeks, Dee Dee was on a tattoo kick. It wouldn't be past 8:00 a.m., and he'd already have me driving to Long Island or Manhattan for tattoos. One day I had an appointment, so he took the train to the lower east side, assuring me that he wouldn't go crazy. Well, when he came home, he had two huge lobsters tattooed on his torso. He displayed them proudly, and I couldn't believe my eyes. "Why on earth would you get two huge lobsters tattooed on your torso?" He got *so* mad and told me that they weren't lobsters—they were scorpions. What the hell? They both looked the same to me. They were huge and looked just like lobsters at first glance.

Before too long, Dee Dee's arms were covered with tattoos. When I first met him, he only had the word "mother" inside of a heart on his upper right arm. Eventually he'd added "Baby Doll" (his nickname for me) with a blonde in a bikini on his right forearm, "Vera & Dee Dee" on his left forearm, a leopard on his upper left arm, lobsters on his torso, and a huge cross on his neck. For every experience he encountered, he got a new tattoo to symbolize the event. His whole life could be defined on his body.

His fantasies with watches were just the same. It was always either a new tattoo or a new watch or another piece of jewelry or some kind of shopping—every morning! Once Dee Dee made up his mind about something, he *had* to have it; this was a daily occurrence. If he was sober for any length of time, his other addictions would surface and continue on to another extreme. Despite Dee Dee's many addictions, it soon became apparent to me that I myself had become an addict. I was addicted to Dee Dee, and he was my drug! Somewhere down the line this chain would need to be broken—but when?

Finally, we were to go to Canada for a few shows. So we arrived in Toronto where we spent three days for some gigs. Toronto is a lovely city, and on our first day we went to a popular Indian restaurant and saw a new James Bond movie that had just come out. Even though I was never fond of Indian cuisine in the beginning, by the time we had spent three months touring England, Scotland, and Ireland, I had grown to love Indian cuisine. It was always a big treat for us.

Before we had left New York to head to Toronto, Dr. Finkle—Dee Dee's psychiatrist at the time—had changed his medication and incorporated Lithium into his regular doses of several other medications, including Thorazine. Within a two-week period we started to notice massive amounts of black hair on Dee Dee's pillows in the morning, which concerned us very much. Being a bald rockstar was not fashionable then, and being a bald Ramone was *not* an image the band would approve of.

One morning he woke up and was experiencing a side effect of one of the drugs (probably the Stelazine, an anti-psychotic medication, and Lithium combined was the most likely culprit). He said then, and reiterated all day long, that he felt really intense, like he was jumping out of his skin. The name of the hotel we were staying at has slipped my mind, but it was quite fancy. We were on a high floor, at least ten floors up. There we had a balcony where we would smoke so the smell didn't go out into the hallway. Out of nowhere, Dee Dee told me that he couldn't shake the feeling of the drugs and that he was going to jump off of the balcony. He said the drug was making him jump out of his skin, and he couldn't help himself. This continued for several hours until I had to physically restrain him from jumping off of the balcony by holding his pant legs down. The whole episode was totally exhausting for both of us, emotionally and physically.

I pleaded and tried to reason with him, but he kept trying to throw himself over the balcony to put himself out of his misery. Oh, my God, what more could I do? I called his doctor in New York, and his response to the hair loss was, "Do you want a bald, sane husband or a mentally ill one with hair?" Well, this was not an acceptable answer as far as I was concerned. If Dee Dee hadn't made his livelihood onstage, the bald part wouldn't have bothered me so much—I'd *love* him anyway. But when I told the doctor about the whole balcony business, he finally understood that there were indications that the Lithium combined with the Stelazine and Thorazine was having some horrible repercussions! He agreed to have the medications' doses lowered, but us being out of the country was a problem. Somehow, we managed to arrange to change his doses with a nearby pharmacist and within two or three days, Dee Dee was back to normal. Normal for Dee Dee, that is!

It was while on our tour of Canada that I had found out I was pregnant. My test came back positive. I didn't know how Dee Dee would react, and at first I was afraid to tell him, but he was overjoyed and vowed to change once and for all. We were already picking out baby names: *Ramona? Sheena? Tiffany?* We didn't even know if it was going to be a girl. But a little "Dee Dee" would have been just as cool. For two months we hid the secret because we were afraid to tell John. He hated kids, and God only knew what he would say or think about me being pregnant. Ramones aren't supposed to have kids, and a baby crying on the bus would never be tolerated.

Despite that, we looked forward to having a baby, although I certainly had my concerns about raising a child in an environment full of drama and unexpected twists and turns. I could hardly handle what I had to deal with, let alone a baby. *Was it fair to bring a baby into such unforeseeable surroundings?* I really was afraid that one night he would come home after a show, possibly in a foul rage or drugged out, and maybe harm the baby. If the baby was crying in the middle of the night after Dee Dee came home from a show, I wouldn't want him to throw it on the floor like he used to do with the lamps. All kinds of crazy scenarios went through my head! I was scared. Dee Dee demanded my attention at all times. Our life revolved around him, his moods, his needs, his demands, his band, and how could I do both? I really didn't think he could take a backseat to a baby; he relied on me for everything. I wasn't Superwoman! *He* was my baby! I had deep concerns, but it turned out that I never made it through my first trimester. It was probably the daily stress and extreme highs and lows I was experiencing that contributed to my losing the baby.

Dee Dee and I cried and held each other and consoled one another as best as we could under the circumstances. I guess God knew what he was doing, and I *suppose* it was for the best. We were extremely disappointed, but there was nothing left to do but accept the reality that it wasn't meant to be. At least we didn't have to tell John the news, and that was a big relief. It's sad that we even had to worry about telling him in the first place.

I remember that a few months before, I had had a conversation with Tina Weymouth in L.A. while she was touring with the Talking Heads and was six months pregnant with her first child with Chris Frantz. We were lying poolside at the Sunset Marquis Hotel, and she talked openly to me like a true friend about how having a baby with Dee Dee would really change our relationship—our focus would be more on the child than on Dee Dee. I listened wholeheartedly and appreciated her kind words and advice, but deep down I had my doubts.

I thought long and hard about that conversation but was still willing to give it a try even after telling Tina how the band would feel about having a baby around. She was well aware of what my concerns were and where I was coming from. She knew the band well, as they had traveled together in the earlier years, and she knew what a full plate I had. But Dee Dee and I had just started to come around and accept that a little Ramone was going to be a part of our lives when our dream was shattered once again. We were extremely disappointed with the outcome.

"The Fuehrer," Joey's "Angela," and "Crazy Phil"

John bullied everyone, and Dee Dee was cautious of John's wrath. At various times he would pick on certain people, who would be given "the treatment" and were forced to endure his meanness. He always picked different people on different tours, and even though John did not do drugs, he entertained himself in this way. He amused himself and kept everyone around him in control. John's controlling behavior drove Dee Dee crazy and into vicious rages to the point where he wanted to kill him. But everyone went along with the whole control thing. No one dared to go against the Fuehrer, so you really didn't speak your mind and kept your opinions to yourself—for your own good.

In a sick sort of way John's control thing empowered him at the expense of others—it was entertainment for him. Towards the end, Dee Dee could no longer tolerate this, and it was one of the main reasons why he eventually left the band. Each Ramone had his own unique and distinct personality and together they were quite an eclectic group of people. Not one of them was ever ordinary, and this is what made them stand apart from other bands. They were all original! Things had become so tense when the band was together; we were not the happy family their fans imagined. After numerous years of deep-rooted grudges, the band did not speak to each other offstage and certainly did not socialize together. There was so much hostility and resentment between them that they couldn't even pick up their hotel-room keys at the front desk together. They wouldn't walk out of the bus together or eat across from each other in small restaurants or truck stops. Johnny would rather sit at the counter than look at anyone else. It got real ugly, and in those days, Dee Dee was like a walking, ticking time bomb. Anything could set him off at any time, and once he exploded there was a dear price to pay for the person at the receiving end. He could be compared to a Category-5 hurricane. Nothing was left standing after Dee Dee came through. Believe me!

By now, Linda had left Joey for Johnny, and since she had to stay behind in New York—because of the tension between Joey and John—she could no longer come on the road or in the van with us. It was no secret that Johnny and Joey hated one another, and it was a miracle the band didn't break up because of that alone. Johnny would make everyone else suffer by indulging himself in his usual sadistic behavior. This devastated Joey, and he was never the same happy guy—until he met Angela.

Angela, originally from California but now living in New York, was Camille's sister, who was Monte's girlfriend at the time. I remember first meeting my new best friend at My Father's Place, a venue out in Roslyn, Long Island, where the Ramones were playing. We immediately hit it off! We had the same interests and sense of humor, and I hadn't seen Joey so happy since before Linda left him for Johnny. Believe it or not, Joey had many girlfriends, but they didn't last long. Angela was different. She looked hot and dressed cool. She even changed her hair color to peroxide blonde at Joey's request. Joey and Angela became a great couple, and they both liked to party—she certainly brought Joey out of his depression. Angela became, and still is to this very day, a good friend of mine. When we were on the road traveling with the band, and the boys were busy doing interviews or record signings, we would shop till we dropped! Literally, we would have to buy extra luggage for all the new clothes we bought in London on Kings Road because it simply couldn't fit in our existing bags. We loved shopping there, especially at stores like Vivienne Westwood's SEX. Both Angela and I have wonderful memories of those days. And living with a Ramone was something only a few of us in this world could relate to.

The day-to-day, city-to-city, country-to-country tours were always filled with plenty of excitement and drama. We had a blast together, but like everything, all good things come to an end. Angela and Joey lived together for several years. Even after their separation they remained close, and he often visited her and her daughter Raven (from another relationship) and spent many holidays with them—until his untimely death. Joey was a special person and a very dear friend to me. I will always remember our heart-to-heart talks and support for one another through all the hard times. I miss him dearly.

* * *

During our many travels to various countries we did have our favorite cities. Los Angeles was one we always looked forward to visiting. We usually stayed at the Holiday Inn on Hollywood Boulevard at Highland. We loved L.A. The shows there were always sold out, and it was a major event when the Ramones came to town. There were always celebrities that would come backstage—the band always loved that other rock stars would come to see them after the show. I met Chrissie

Hynde in the audience during one of these shows, and since Dee Dee and I were such big fans of hers, I brought her backstage to meet the band afterwards. She just so happened to be staying at the same hotel as us, the Le Parc Hotel, and we invited her to ride with us on the bus back to the hotel. We really enjoyed meeting her. She was so cool! Members of Blondie such as Clem Burke and Frank Infante would also come backstage, often with members of the Go-Go's. Billy Idol would also show up. Backstage after a Ramones concert was always exciting in Los Angeles; it was where you could see the cream of the crop of rock and roll.

I remember meeting little-girl fans waiting at the backstage door after some of the shows. They would come up to me and tell me that Dee Dee was their favorite Ramone and that he was so cute. They would tell me that I was so-o-o lucky to be his wife. While I smiled graciously at their admiration, I couldn't help thinking to myself, *If they only knew!*

London was another favorite place of ours! After the show there in 1987 there was a special private party held for the Ramones at the Embassy, which was the hot new club at the time. It didn't take long for Dee Dee to befriend Phil Lynot from Thin Lizzy, known mostly for their big hit "The Boys Are Back In Town." Phil seemed likable enough and pretty harmless, but it quickly became apparent that he and Dee Dee had more in common than just music. Soon enough Phil was giving heroin to Dee Dee to sniff privately in the bathroom. I wasn't sure why exactly they were going to the bathroom so often, so I asked our pal Lemmy from Motorhead to find out what was happening in there, because Dee Dee had actually been sober for ninety days. The next thing I knew, Lemmy and Phil were having a huge argument over Phil giving Dee Dee heroin.

That wasn't even the whole picture. Phil kept telling me throughout the night how Dee Dee and I should go back to his flat after the party, and then he started telling me about certain sexual things he liked to do. I was like, "What the fuck are you talking about?" He told Dee Dee he had more stuff at the house, and Dee Dee was looking forward to going there and doing more drugs after the party. What Phil wasn't telling him was that he planned on having a three-way! No fucking way were we going there. Dee Dee had no idea what was going on. He was completely out of it and on another planet. I frantically looked for Monte and told him that he had to get us a cab immediately, and he had to help me get Dee Dee—incoherent by now—out of there and back to our hotel ASAP!

Once the cab came, I grabbed Dee Dee quickly and told him we were going to Phil's house as we were getting into the cab. He gladly jumped in, but instead I had the cab driver take us back to our hotel at the Kensington Hilton. By the time we had gotten to the hotel he was totally confused. I was just relieved that we were finally out of that place. The whole evening was crazy, to say the least, but now we were safe, and the worst was over—until next time anyway.

Nevertheless, Dee Dee lost his ninety days of sobriety, and it was always a challenge to start over again. So, by this point he was off the wagon again, and it always took a while until he could get himself back on track. Sobriety was a constant daily struggle, but Dee Dee had an especially addictive personality and could not do drugs socially (if there was such a thing). For him it was always a "Do or Die" situation; there was no medium ground. He was like an alcoholic who can't have a drink socially without drinking the whole bottle and getting full-blown drunk!

In the morning we went down to the hotel restaurant for a full breakfast buffet that was included in the price of our room. To my amazement Duran Duran was also staying there and having breakfast as well. Wow! I couldn't believe there was Simon LeBon right next to me and Nick Rhodes, who had on more makeup than me at seven o'clock in the morning. But *they* were in awe of Dee Dee Ramone! They all acknowledged Dee Dee as we filled our plates and sat down to have a great breakfast. They were quite friendly to Dee Dee, and he loved it. It was totally awesome.

CHAPTER FIFTEEN

Ramones Don't Rap

By 1987 Dee Dee was completely into the rap movement that was taking the country by storm. Even though Blondie had done "Rapture" much earlier, rap just got bigger and bigger. By the late '80s, Dee Dee was rhyming all over the house. He made everything rhyme and I'd rhyme back! He tried to incorporate the new rap music into the Ramones' songs, but Johnny would have none of it: "What are you thinking? We are the Ramones. The Ramones don't do rap!" That was when Dee Dee started to accumulate a few songs on his own and became so inspired by the rappers of the time, people like the Beastie Boys, Run DMC, LL Cool J, Dough E. Fresh, Loudmouth, Salt-N-Pepa, Public Enemy, Jazzy Jeff and Fresh Prince just to name a few.

I was always supportive of any fresh new ideas that Dee Dee would come up with and tried to encourage him to express his feelings through his lyrics and his songwriting. I remember he was in Texas doing a few dates with the Ramones when he called me at home and rapped me something he had written in the van, while they were driving from city to city. It was called "Funky Man." I thought it was great and encouraged him to keep working on it. Writing songs or lyrics or keeping daily journals was a sort of therapy for him. It got his mind off of looking for drugs and getting into trouble. It turned any negative energy he harbored into a positive result. Just like

Ramones' songs that were written and performed with a distinct sound and phrasing, Dee Dee's rapping was not the usual rap either. The Ramones' songs and the rap songs had different sounds completely, but Dee Dee's writing and sense of humor were still apparent and came through regardless.

He would play his new songs for Richie Ramone, and Richie would also give him positive feedback. It was all positive, so it was all good, and it gave Dee Dee a new avenue to explore and in which to reinvent himself, through a different kind of music. He needed to do this; he didn't want to be labeled a *pinhead* anymore, but the Ramones would not allow him to grow musically as an artist. In the band, he felt stifled and compelled to write the same stuff over and over again. He needed an out, and so "Dee Dee King" was born. Dee Dee Ramone became also known as Dee Dee King.

It was Richie Ramone's wife, Annette Stark, who introduced Dee Dee and me to Chris Williamson. He was the owner of Rock Hotel Records, a label distributed by Profile Records at the time. Chris listened to "Funky Man" and thought it would make a great single. Since the Ramones would not let Dee Dee put out anything under the name Dee Dee Ramone that was not a Ramones song or punk music, he had to come up with another name. He had just written the title song for Stephen King's *Pet Semetary*, and we both were such *huge* fans of King, it was a no-brainer that Dee Dee would call himself "Dee Dee King." This way the Ramones would not be embarrassed by Dee Dee using the "Ramone" name to do rap. We were so excited that a single would be coming out, and the label also wanted a Dee Dee King video to follow. Everyone loved the "aka Dee Dee King" name, and the response was very favorable. He just threw his whole heart into the new persona that he'd developed. It was all very exciting.

Dee Dee always stated that Stephen King was his hero and was the "King" of books and movies. Dee Dee considered himself King of Punk. He was a narcissist and everything, everyday, revolved around Dee Dee because he thought he really was the *king*. If he wasn't writing rap songs or playing Ramones' shows, in his spare time he would play with his switchblades and read *How to Kill* books. The books, which I still have in my possession, covered topics from Tai Kwon Do to nunchucks as weapons to various other ways to use deadly force and hand-to-hand combat. He would take karate lessons and practice these deadly maneuvers all over the house, and he even learned the particular points on the human body that were the most vulnerable (should an occasion arise where he would need to use such information). He was obsessed with killing, but I never even saw him kill a single cockroach in all the years I was with him. Just knowing these things gave him a sense of empowerment that played a big part in his kingly self-image.

Dee Dee was a very unique individual who had numerous personas and could adapt different characteristics and make them his own. They say there is a fine line between genius and insanity: Dee Dee lived on the edge, and that is what made him the legend that he is today. The man was a complicated individual, but that was what inspired him every morning when he woke up; that was what made him tick. This was Dee Dee—he was a psycho-rocker, but he was also a genius with a heart of gold, a very sensitive and kind-hearted human being. *This* was the Dee Dee that I knew and loved. He was actually tri-polar.

"Funky Man" was Dee Dee's first solo project. We both worked really hard on it and started Baby Doll

Productions, named after the rap name that Dee Dee had given me: Baby Doll King. His new project was a lot of fun for the both of us. After "Funky Man" had been recorded, the next step was making a video to accompany the song. We also contacted artist James Rizzi and commissioned him to do the artwork for the album cover, front and back, for the twelve-inch single. The concept was based on the lyrics to the song, and he did an incredible job. We absolutely *loved* it. His design was so Dee Dee! The day arrived to film the video, and part of it was to be shot in Arturo Vega's loft and the rest in an East Village garage completely covered in graffiti down on Avenue B. Lots of fans had gathered, and we even had our small, white Mercedes 380 SL convertible—which Dee Dee loved—in the video. It was a long, hard day, but it was also a lot of fun. Arturo was always very helpful and willing to do anything he could for anyone in the band. He was a big part of the Ramones family and a tremendous asset.

When the first Dee Dee King single came out, MTV only played it about three times, and it was not promoted at all. The single was not well received. The band wanted the single to flop. They knew if it was unsuccessful, Dee Dee would not leave, and he would continue writing Ramones songs about geeks and freaks, pinheads and warthogs. But this did not deter Dee Dee. He was even more into rap than ever before; with "Funky Man" he was basically just getting his feet wet. So every morning, and all day long, he would write lyrics and music. At night I would drop him off at Daniel Rey's house to work on new songs, and the next morning we would listen to the demos over and over again.

He wrote a version of "Mash Potato Time" and asked Debbie Harry to sing some back-up vocals. When

Dee Dee backstage after a Ramones show in the late 1970s.
Photo by George Bennett

Monte A. Melnick, Dee Dee Ramone, and L.A. DJ Rodney Bingenheimer backstage at the Starwood in Hollywood, August 16, 1976.
Photo © Jenny Lens Punk Archive/Cache Agency

Dee Dee and Joey Ramone performing at the Savoy in San Francisco, August 20, 1976.
Photo © Jenny Lens Punk Archive/Cache Agency

Backstage at the Sunset Strip's famous Whisky a Go Go, October 21, 1977: Dee Dee with Joan Jett, a guitarist for The Runaways at the time.
Photo © Jenny Lens Punk Archive/Cache Agency

Dee Dee Ramone with writer Pleasant Gehman (L) and noted L.A. punk icon Hellin Killer (R) backstage at the Whisky, October 21, 1977.
Photo © Jenny Lens Punk Archive/Cache Agency

Dee Dee onstage at the Starwood, 1976.
Photo © Jenny Lens Punk Archive/ Cache Agency

The Ramones onstage, 1978.
From the Vera Ramone King collection

Dee Dee performing onstage, 1978.
Photo by George Bennett

Danny Fields, first Ramones' manager in 1977.
Photo by Godlis

(L-R) Joey Ramone, The Ramones' artistic director Arturo Vega, Dee Dee Ramone, 1976.
Photo © Jenny Lens Punk Archive/Cache Agency

Original lyrics by
Dee Dee.
From the Vera Ramone
King collection

nobody gives a damn about me
nobody cares about a junkie

gotta do what I gotta do
I might have to pull a gun on you
gotta do what I gotta do to survive
gotta hundred dollar a day habit to keep alive

Dee Dee performing onstage
during the Ramones' European
tour, September, 1978.
Photo by Kees Tabak

The Ramones' life on
the road
Photo by Kees Tabak

Dee Dee backstage with his classic white Fender bass guitars in Amsterdam, 1978.
Photo by Kees Tabak

The Ramones playing for fans in California.
Photo courtesy of Ariola-Sire

An animated Dee Dee.
Photo by Ian Harper

Vera at a photo shoot with famed New
York photographer Keith Green.

Dee Dee and Vera in their Whitestone, Queens, apartment.
Photo by George Bennett

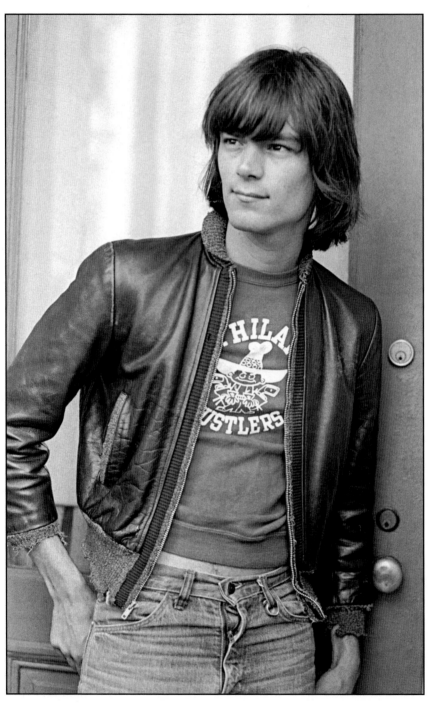

Dee Dee Ramone at Aquarius Records, San Francisco, August 20, 1976.
Photo © Jenny Lens Punk Archive/Cache Agency

Vera Ramone in her custom-made, punk-rock, studded bra-top.
Photo by Bob Gruen

(L-R) Joey, Linda Stein, David Bowie, Dee Dee, Danny Fields, and Vera Ramone at the Mudd Club.
Photo by Bob Gruen

Rock legends. (L-R) Joey Ramone, Tommy Ramone, Iggy Pop, Seymour Stein, Seymour Stein, Linda Stein, Lenny Kaye, Dee Dee Ramone and Johnny Ramone.
Photo by Roberta Bayley

Dee Dee King showing off his new tattoo.
Photo by Bob Gruen

Dee Dee in action.
Photo by Kees Tabak

Randy's Roadhouse sound check.
Photo by Lindell Tate

Vera and
Dee Dee at
the "Funkyman"
video shoot.
From the Vera
Ramone King
collection

Dee Dee during the shoot.
From the Vera Ramone King
collection

Dee Dee King accessories: belt, jewelry, sneakers, rap chains.
Photo by Bob Gruen

Dee Dee's A. A. Serenity Prayer.
From the Vera Ramone King collection

God grant us the serenity to accept the things we cannot change the courage to change the things we can and the wisdom to know the difference

A Dee Dee King promo picture.
Photo by Bob Gruen

Baby Doll King.

Baby Doll

I am a man in love with a pure heart
someone above sent me a work of art
the happyness I feel
is so very real
you smiled at me and I sat down and cryed
and on that day all the evil in me died
I don't care what I used to do
that wasn't realy me
how can I thank you

Ba-a-a-by Doll
Ba-a-a-by Doll
I will allways love you Baby Doll

we walked down the aile and made a bond
the sculpter waved his magic wand
and created a work of art
you and I will never part
and now your willing to give me a child
On one condition I stop running wild
you taught me to stand tall
you are my Baby Doll

you are my goddess
and god has blessed the two of us

as consistant as the heavens
I know I can last
even I can survive
I just gotta think fast

theres all this temptation
drugs are allways the blame
runken through the fire
burnnen in the flame

the morning is damp
from last nights rain
I change my life
but it still stays the same

I've got to start over again
and I know dam well
where I got to begin
I've got to become Super Man

I got to demand
that somthing change
runnen through the fire
burnnen in the flame

Handwritten lyrics to "Baby Doll."
From the Vera Ramone King collection

Never-released lyrics by Dee Dee Ramone.
From the Vera Ramone King collection

GERMAN KID ①

THis is Dee Dee King
on the mike
150 pounds
oF Dynmite
the guy with the ryme
About the pyrmioe
bet you oiont know
I was a german kio
uno ich Finde es gut
wenn leute lacht
ich habe die energie
ich habe die kraft
ein huebshes Maedchen
gibt mir ein kuss
kein Geld Fur den taxi
nehm den Bus
ich bin der koenig
Von mein haus
wenn die kinder
sino zu laut
schrei ich
Den raus

Handwritten lyrics to "German Kid."
From the Vera Ramone King collection

②

well I useD to be A German kio
stanoen on the street
with two cents in my pocket
Ano nothen to eat
did you ever see a glider
soaren in the wind
bet you didnt know
I was halF German
Ano Iam doen Rap
not Bethoven
yea Iam doen Rap
ano Ive just begun
es ist mir egal
was du sagst
ich mach eine Party
jeden Tag
ich hab immer
sehr viel Glueck
Dee Dee King
ist nicht verrueckt

③

you wouldnt Believe
the places Ive been
its pretty cool
to be halF German
slap me Five
gimmie some skin
I useo to live
in Berlin
ich lese die Zeitung
jeoen tag
was is Das Für Musik
die Eltern Frag
Zetz hab ich
genug gesagt
auF ▬▬▬▬ Wiedersehen
guten NAcht
ich Finde es gut
wenn leute lacht
lacht

HAlF American
HAlF German
HAlF American
HAlF German

A love letter that Dee Dee, "Bunny," wrote to Vera during the Ramones' stay at a San Antonio La Quinta in January, 1979.

From the Vera Ramone King collection

Dee Dee, doing what he loved to do most.
Photo by George Bennett

Dee Dee, performing onstage, 1988-89.
Photo by Ian Harper

Joey, Johnny, Marky, Dee Dee: The Ramones. Milan, 1989.
From the Vera Ramone King collection

Dee Dee, standing on the balcony of New York's famous Chelsea Hotel, 1993.

In memory of the Ramones' longtime manager Gary Kurfirst. R.I.P.
Photo by Shawn Chadwick

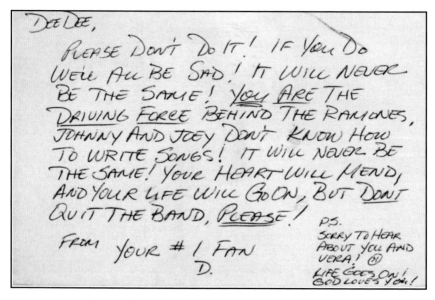

DEE DEE,
PLEASE DON'T DO IT! IF YOU DO
WE'LL ALL BE SAD! IT WILL NEVER
BE THE SAME! YOU ARE THE
DRIVING FORCE BEHIND THE RAMONES,
JOHNNY AND JOEY DON'T KNOW HOW
TO WRITE SONGS! IT WILL NEVER BE
THE SAME! YOUR HEART WILL MEND,
AND YOUR LIFE WILL GO ON, BUT DON'T
QUIT THE BAND, PLEASE!
FROM YOUR #1 FAN
D.

P.S.
SORRY TO HEAR
ABOUT YOU AND
VERA!
LIFE GOES ON!
GOD LOVES YOU!

A postcard sent to Dee Dee by a fan after he left the band.
From the Vera Ramone King collection

Vera and Dee Dee hanging out in Arturo Vega's loft, 1980-81.
From the Vera Ramone King collection

Dee Dee and Vera after a Ramones show.
From the Vera Ramone King collection

A fan's eye-view: Dee Dee and Vera Ramone.
From the Vera Ramone King collection

Dee Dee and Vera, punk royalty, at the MTV Awards in 1986.
Photo by Bob Gruen

At the opening of The Sanctuary, a famous club in Manhattan.
Photo by Eileen Polk

At an after-hours club in the mid-1980s. (L-R) Bass guitarist Busta Jones, Arturo Vega, Dee Dee, and Vera.
From the Vera Ramone King collection

Dee Dee and one of his custom guitars.
From the Vera Ramone King collection

The happy couple at home together on Christmas Day, 1989.
From the Vera Ramone King collection

Christmas time with (L-R) Dee Dee, his sister Beverly, her
husband Joe, Grandma, and Mom, Toni.
From the Vera Ramone King collection

Vera in her leopard-print jacket
and Dee Dee in leather.
From the Vera Ramone King collection

Happy Anniversary card from
"Bunny" to Vera.

Too many pills.

Front cover of "Funkyman". Artwork by James Rizzi. *From the Vera Ramone King collection*

Back cover of "Funkyman". Artwork by James Rizzi. *From the Vera Ramone King collection*

Joey, Raven, and Angela on Easter morning late 1990s.
From the Vera Ramone King collection

Dee Dee being Dee Dee.
Photo by Frank Granada

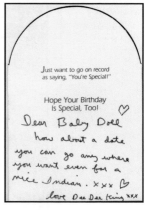

Just want to go on record
as saying, "You're Special!"

Hope Your Birthday
Is Special, Too!

Dear Baby Doll
how about a date
you can go any where
you want even for a
nice Indian. xxx
love Dee Dee King xxx

Happy Birthday, Baby Doll:
"...you can go anywhere you
want even for a nice Indian
(meal)."

1996, Coney Island High: The last NYC Ramones show. (L-R) Michael Alargo, Joey Ramone, Linda Stein, Dee Dee Ramone, Arturo Vega, Kevin Patrick.
Photo by Jimmy Marino

1996, The Palace in Los Angeles: The last Ramones show. (L-R) Jimmy Marino, Chris Cornell, Joey Ramone, Dee Dee Ramone, Arturo Vega.
Photo by Jimmy Marino

1998 at "LIFE" club in NYC. Dee Dee Ramone, Keith Richards, Daniel Rey: mutual admirers.
Photo by Jimmy Marino

Taken backstage at a Chesterfield Kings show in Hoboken, NJ, 1988-89.
From the Vera Ramone King collection

Vera and her soon-to-be husband Kenny in the early 1990s.
From the Vera Ramone King collection

Dee Dee King: *Standing in the Spotlight.*
Photos by Bob Gruen

The rock wife.

Vera, smiling through the storm.

Dee Dee at home with his dog during happier times.

Marky, Vera, and Marian Ramone in July, 2007.
From the Vera Ramone King collection

Ramones' fan "Dr. Dot" with Vera in 1984.
Photo Courtesy of Dot Stein

Dee Dee's and Vera's passport photos from the late 1980s.
From the Vera Ramone King collection

A relaxed Joey, Richie, and Dee Dee having piña coladas in Miami Beach, 1987.
From the Vera Ramone King collection

Vera and Linda Drake at the Hollywood Forever Cemetery in 2007.
From the Vera Ramone King collection

Vera and Kenny in an upstate New York gift shop in 1991.
From the Vera Ramone King collection

Arturo Vega, considered by many to be the "5th Ramone," with his friend Lisa Brownie at Los Angeles' Key Club in 2008.
Photo by Fernando Guerrero

he wrote "German Kid," he also had Chris Stein play guitar on the song. Debbie and Chris were always so accommodating to Dee Dee, and Debbie especially was always available to help him out. I admired her and thought she was so beautiful. She was the ultimate Punk Rock Queen and was my idol. She was a rock icon, even way back then. There was only one Debbie Harry. I recently saw a picture of her in *Star Magazine* wearing a Dee Dee King T-shirt for "Standing in the Spotlight," which was a limited edition and collector's item. She still looked as stunning as ever. She always had an incredibly beautiful face. It was an honor to have Debbie and Chris be a part of Dee Dee's solo album.

Not deterred by his early critics, Dee Dee continued writing frantically every day and soon had more than enough songs for a full-length album. There was one song called "Baby Doll" that he wrote for me. It was a special song that expressed not only his innermost feelings and gratitude but also how much he loved me and how much I meant to him. When he first played that song for me, we both cried. It was a moment that I'll never forget. Dee Dee did display a lot of crazy behavior, but he was also deep and sensitive and loving. We were very much in love for a long time, but he wasn't the easiest person to live with. He was compulsive, impulsive, and outrageous. Other than that he was a lot of fun and very lovable. We had many great times together. You could say I was his Sharon Osbourne. I kept him grounded yet let him be himself.

Daniel Rey worked with him on his Dee Dee King album and produced it. Once Seymour Stein heard "Baby Doll" he agreed to release the album on Sire Records. Dee Dee and I were ecstatic, but the Ramones were less than thrilled. None of them had ever had a solo project apart from the band, and this did not sit well with them, especially Johnny. One day, Dee Dee showed up at rehearsal in his full rap regalia, an expensive brand-name sweat suit, Adidas sneakers with about ten pounds of gold-wrap chains around his neck, and a gold-and-diamond ring on every finger. When Monte picked him up at the house he told him John was going to have a fit! I had also warned him that there were going to be repercussions when he saw him. But Dee Dee did as Dee Dee wanted, and he was certainly up for the challenge.

It was as though he was a schoolboy, going against all the rules and just being defiant and rebellious. When he finally got to rehearsal and Johnny saw him, Dee Dee just glared back, daring him to say one word. Johnny rolled his eyes in disgust and mumbled something under his breath. He had known Dee Dee a long time and knew well enough when to back off. He knew that Dee Dee was like an explosive time bomb waiting to be set off. Dee Dee would have been ready to kill and go to combat if necessary. No one was going to tell him what to do—ever!

CHAPTER SIXTEEN

Too Tough to Die

Some people may have thought that I was too controlling. But on the contrary, it was Dee Dee who was the controller. Dee Dee was his own worst enemy, he was an extremist with everything he did, and I just tried to keep him from going overboard. Living like this became normal for us after a while. If we hadn't loved each other, we would have never overcome all the adversities that we survived. He could be a real pain in the ass when he wanted to, and there were very few people that he would consider the voice of reason.

The band did not really approve of Dee Dee doing his own solo project, but there was little they could do to stop him. I think Joey secretly felt that if Dee Dee could break the ice and do his own thing, then one day he could also have his own project. Making Dee Dee's solo album, which he named *Standing in the Spotlight*, was really a big job, and everyday there was a lot to do besides Dee Dee writing all of the songs, roughly fifteen or sixteen demos. My job was to design the album cover, front and back, get all his rap outfits together for his approval, and arrange for Bob Gruen to do the photo session. Later, we sifted through the pictures and picked out the ones suitable for the eventual album cover.

All of this work and energy kept him focused, and besides smoking the best pot (almost an ounce a day), he was preoccupied with creating something positive instead of being self-destructive. So, at the end of the day, it was all good. By this time, Marky Ramone had rejoined the band after taking some time off to concentrate on his own sobriety. He became a member of Alcoholics Anonymous, which gave Dee Dee someone else in the band who would attend AA meetings with him while they were on the road. They would have short AA meetings together before the shows, and this was a good thing; Marky became his true friend. So it was only natural that Marky—who played drums—would be the only Ramone asked to play on Dee Dee's solo album. Eventually ten of the best songs were picked and recording sessions were scheduled to begin at Chung King Studios in Chinatown, where a lot of other rappers also recorded. The album, produced and cowritten by Daniel Rey, was not your typical rap-sounding album. It was given the term "rap and roll." It was a clever and different-sounding album, but it was totally Dee Dee, and the lyrics and flavor described his sense of humor to a tee. It was a novelty album more than a rap album. It was certainly never meant to be taken as a *serious* rap album. Most people just didn't get it. It was supposed to be fun! *Billboard* magazine actually gave it a very favorable review.

Dee Dee was extremely clever and prolific as far as constantly coming up with new songs. That was all he had to do: write, create, and perform. I took care of all the rest. In all of our years together, Dee Dee never even had to change as much as a lightbulb—he would probably opt for buying a new fixture instead. Some of his greatest hits were "53rd & 3rd," "Rockaway Beach," "Chinese Rocks," "Commando," "Too Tough To Die," "Something To Believe In," "I Believe In Miracles," and so many more. People of his caliber don't come around but once in a lifetime. He was genuinely a good person but a slave to his own demons. He just couldn't shake them, and eventually, they consumed him.

It was during this time, in the winter and spring of 1989, that I started to experience excruciating headaches that would last 24/7 for weeks straight. I went to several doctors, but they couldn't find a reason or explanation for the headaches and would prescribe pills that didn't do a damn thing for me. Finally, one doctor suggested that I see a psychiatrist—that it was all in my head! I started to think that maybe Dee Dee's sickness was rubbing off on me after twelve years: Could I have caught it? Despite everything, I started seeing a woman therapist in Bayside, Queens. She put me on Prozac, but I still had the headaches.

Dee Dee's album was released in the spring, and despite some interviews and record signings, there wasn't really much promotion, and the record sales were dismal at best. The album was D.O.A. This was a depressing time for Dee Dee; on top of his album's poor performance, a real estate investment we had made earlier had gone under. These were tough times for us, and he became increasingly difficult with each passing day. Even a half dozen baths, an ounce of weed, and two AA meetings a day weren't enough!

Dee Dee was a perfectionist when it came to his work, and this was a big blow. Nothing was good enough, and it became obvious that he was having a mental breakdown at this point. He also told me that he wanted to quit the Ramones. "What? Your solo album flopped, and you want to leave the band? And do what? How are we going to live? How can we afford to pay our bills?" There were several issues that were mounting with every passing day, like a volcano getting ready to erupt. Dee Dee would joke about playing the accordion in Central Park with the monkey on his shoulder or being a doorman in a Fifth Avenue building.

One day he got all dressed up in his leather pants with seven watches on one arm, his ten gold rings, and at least fifteen pounds of rap chains hanging from his neck, on top of all his tattoos covering most of his body. I asked him point-blank, "And where do you think you're going?" He said that his friends, Barry and Jeff from AA, were coming to pick him up to go to a meeting. He said he needed one. After being together for so many years, I could tell that trouble was around the corner, and the bomb was ticking. Besides all of this, for some reason I just wasn't feeling well and had to lie down a lot because of my headaches. I was tired all the time, and all the stress was really getting to me. I didn't know what to expect next.

One afternoon a while later, I came home from doing some errands, and I noticed Dee Dee starting to have a seizure in the living room. I didn't know what, if anything, he could have taken while I was out, and I started to freak out. Soon he was foaming at the mouth and was incoherent. His eyes were rolling back in his head while I proceeded to dial 911, and an ambulance came in no less than five minutes. They took him to the hospital where they pumped his stomach. Apparently he had poisoned himself by drinking alcohol. He had been taking Antabuse daily, among other anti-psychotic medications, and thought that since he didn't take his Antabuse for a few days, he could have a drink. Not true! Those anti-psychotic drugs do not work that way. They stay in your system for thirty days before you can have a drink. Either this was never explained to him properly, or he had forgotten and decided to have a drink. After I came home I found several little bottles of booze that he had smuggled into the house. He had waited for the opportune time to intoxicate himself and thought that no one would know. He literally poisoned himself in the house while I was out.

After the stomach pumping incident they released him, and, boy, was he in a foul mood. By now, I had become an expert at plastering holes in the wall, sanding them down and repainting them. It became routine. Dee Dee was literally his own worst enemy: He had an extremely self-destructive personality, fueled by an overpowering, uncontrollable inner rage. Out of love, loyalty, and a misguided sense of protectiveness, I tried to cover for him, but his foul moods were becoming more and more frequent and unpredictable. Things could be wonderful one minute, and the next minute he would be ranting and raving with his hands up in the air like a lunatic for no apparent reason. He was always the victim, and everyone else was against him.

* * *

It was May of 1989 when he left to go on a tour of Italy and Greece. I stayed behind to recuperate from the last two drama-filled months. I desperately needed some down time. He came home from this trip in a particularly good mood. He brought me home a gold watch and a beautiful ring—lots of presents! The ring was stunning. It was an 18k-gold ring shaped like a dolphin, with two diamonds for the eyes, and the whole tail that went around the finger was encrusted with red rubies. In Greece, the dolphin symbolizes true love forever and that is why he said he had chosen this particular ring for me. Besides, it was absolutely gorgeous. I totally loved it. That ring was very dear to me.

After his long trip home we decided it might be nice to go to our home in the country for a few days and get some well-deserved R&R. We were barely there half a day when he demanded that we return to the city immediately. I thought, *Not this shit again!* But, oh, yes! I saw the look on his face—he looked like the devil himself—and I was scared. He looked absolutely possessed, and by this point I had seen this look too many times to know that he meant business. He saw that I was scared, and this empowered him even more. I packed up our stuff and drove towards the main highway, without either of us saying a word. I was afraid if I said one wrong thing that this would escalate to something god-awful, and we were in the middle of nowhere.

Halfway home he informed me that I was to drive him straight to the city to 10th Street where he could go cop some hard drugs. Again I said, "I'll drive us home, and if you want to go get dope, get it on your own!" Well, I should have known better than to fuck with Dee Dee Ramone. No sooner than these words rolled off my tongue, when he had a switchblade pointed toward my neck. I just kept quiet and drove, barely able to see the road ahead of me through all the tears running down my face. Out of sheer fear for my life, I did as I was told while the knife was pointed at me. It seemed like an eternity. The minute he got out of the car on 10th Street and turned the corner, I took off and left him there. My heart was beating so fast, and my brain was on overdrive. I headed straight for my sister's house on 9th Street and Third Avenue, fearing for my safety and my life. Little did I know that this was the beginning of the end. I didn't go home that night, and he stayed out all night too.

Our next conversation took place by phone one and a half days later. I told him I needed some time to think about us and needed to be alone. He informed me that if I didn't return home immediately, there would be consequences to pay. When I didn't show up, he went to the bank, cleaned out our account, and headed straight to the city. I didn't hear from him for a couple of days and could not reach him, so I finally went home and waited for the inevitable. He called me and said he was in California at Joel's house (his friend and the best man at our wedding). He also informed me that he had stopped taking all his medications, because he was convinced they were making him fat, and that he was quitting the Ramones.

I pleaded with him to come to his senses, but it fell on deaf ears. His mind was made up, and either I was on board with his decision or *this was it*. We had had many arguments and several splits in the past years, but I knew that this time something was different…. It was over.

CHAPTER SEVENTEEN

The Beginning of the End

By this time my family and close group of friends had grown accustomed to our lifestyle and Dee Dee's unstableness, and to everyone else this was just another fight, another reason for him to binge and go crazy. In my heart, I knew that this time was different. And if he refused to go back on his medications, there would be no "us" in the future. To live with him otherwise would be sheer suicide. He could explode at any moment on me! I was not going to let us be the next version of Sid and Nancy, and I would not become a victim of his uncontrollable rage. He understood my terms, but his mind was made up. When he returned to New York a week later, he informed me that he had a new girlfriend—he had only met her two days prior.

How quickly he had moved on and replaced me. In the blink of an eye, life as I knew it for so-o-o many years was now my past, and I didn't know what to do next. Dee Dee further told me that I was to keep all of our possessions, including the two cars, country home, and Queens apartment. He was starting a new life and had gotten himself an apartment on 10th Street in a tenement with a five-floor walk up! In his mind he thought he was leaving me everything, but in reality he left me with a mortgage, an apartment to pay rent on every month, and two cars—and I'd had no income and no job for the last thirteen years! *He* was my full-time job and my life. To make matters worse, he quit the Ramones four weeks later. So then he didn't have an income either.

How could things go so wrong so quickly? My head was spinning, and my heart was aching. We had always worked out our problems before, and I remember one particular time, when Dee Dee was in rehab, during family therapy, that he begged me crying, "Please don't throw me away!" But this is exactly what he had done to me, and never in my wildest dreams did I ever think it would end that way. I wanted nothing more than for us to overcome the challenges we faced, but we failed. When he left me, he took with him my heart and soul and left me with all the pain. I can't say there were no hard feelings. I was hurt, humiliated, heartbroken, and penniless. We were crazy in love, and I still don't know how things soured so quickly. He had been in and out of different rehabs so often—before they were fashionable—but this was even beyond that. This time he didn't want help, and he didn't need any help, thank you! Some people feared he was having a mid-life crisis, but I truly think that he just gave up.

He left for California with the Ramones to play his last few shows. Everyone had tried to talk some sense into him, and he was having none of it. He was like a bull let out of his pen, and everyone could go fuck themselves! By the time he returned home from California, he found out that the money he'd sent his new girlfriend for the rent was spent on something other than the rent, and he beat the living crap out of her. Their relationship had actually survived only six weeks, and he was gone for three of them. Meanwhile, he was calling me day in and day out at all hours, asking me if he could come home.

I remember one particular night when the phone rang at 1:00 a.m. in the morning. It was Dee Dee. He was at a pay phone somewhere on 10th Street standing under a lamppost in the pouring rain, crying, begging, and pleading with me to let him come home. It broke my heart, and I cried with him, but this was the choice he'd made. I had just started to put the pieces back together myself. I had gotten a regular job by now, and I had to be up by 6:00 a.m. to get ready for work. I had other responsibilities and plenty of bills to pay. I told him once more that unless he went back on his medications, he could not come back home, and there would be no future for us. I would be a robot if I said I didn't feel anger, hurt, and moments of embarrassment because of his behavior. Instead of feeling sorry for myself during this difficult time and asking, "Why is this happening to me?" I just accepted it *was* happening! Life was tough, and it was time to put on my helmet. I made myself move on and etch out the next phase of my life and hoped that all the pieces would eventually fall into place. It was just going to take time and a lot of inner strength and determination. The choice was *not* mine. It was made for me.

It broke my heart to say this, but if I had allowed him to come back, how long would it take until he left again? Two days? Two weeks? My heart was not only broken but whatever was left had been smashed into a million pieces. I was tired of him coming in and out of my life like it was a revolving door when things weren't working out for him. I was no longer willing to be a doormat for his convenience. We lived hard. We loved and fought harder, but breaking up was the hardest part for both of us. Every time he called, we'd both get so emotional and cry, but we both knew things were definitely different this time. When you love someone as much as I loved Dee Dee, sometimes you just have to know when to let them go…and I had to set him free.

Not long after he left me and quit the Ramones, I realized that he had thrown away everything he had striven for and worked hard for all of his life. He gave away the unconditional love of the one person who truly loved him during good times and bad. We were more than husband and wife; we were best friends. He left behind all of his worldly possessions, as well as everything that made him happy and the person he had become. He gave all of this up in return for total freedom, no responsibilities, and no control. He had finally liberated himself from life as he knew it. But what he didn't realize was that what he wanted was the beginning of his demise and eventual death.

Without any stability in his life—the stability that had kept him grounded and focused throughout those earlier years—his mental illness was progressing with each passing day. He lived like a vagabond. He became a restless soul, never staying in one place for very long. In his last years, he became a bitter and angry man who hated everyone, especially himself. Life had soured him, and there was no turning back the clock. It had all become bittersweet.

Shortly after leaving the Ramones, he moved in with a girl named Laura. She told me, as did Dee Dee, that she serviced men for a living. While Dee Dee did not particularly care for her choice of profession, it did pay the bills. She would often call me for advice, as he was a handful to deal with, and I actually liked her as a person. I always gave her my best and honest opinion on how to handle him. I wanted him to be happy and not homeless. I remember that first Thanksgiving after we had officially separated. He called me complaining about having to spend the Thanksgiving holiday all alone. He told me that Laura had a client in from out of town, so she had to work and couldn't spend the holiday with him. He actually wanted me to feel sorry for him and invite him to spend the holiday with my family—after all the crap he had just put me through! I politely declined the invitation he was hoping for and reminded him that he had known full well what she did for a living when he met her. It was he alone who made his choices in the last few months.

Despite everyone trying to talk some sense into him, he refused to listen, and now he had to lie in the bed he had made for himself. Just as he had used his switchblade to rip to shreds the new couch Connie had bought for him years ago, in a fit of rage he had done the same exact thing to Laura's newly purchased mattress. It was when she called to complain about it that I told her how he had done the same thing to the couch years before. It was a pattern. Though he didn't rip up our stuff, he did have that penchant for bashing table lamps to bits in the middle of the night. Eventually, even Dee Dee's new, sweet, young wife could not erase his pain. Life had hardened him. After so many years of striving for what he'd already achieved, he just threw it all away. That's what's so sad about the way his life ended, and no one knew this better than him. The damage had been done a long time ago; nothing would change his destiny. He finally succumbed to his self-destructive ways, and there was no turning back this time.

* * *

It was while he was in London during 1991 that he mailed me a bunch of new songs he had written while he was there. He wanted me to have them and asked me what I thought of them, and if I liked them. Throughout all the Ramones' years it was Dee Dee who wrote most of the songs. Joey wrote as well—he and Dee Dee were both extremely talented songwriters—but Johnny refused to do many of Joey's songs. Well, after so many years together it was extremely hard to talk to Dee Dee like he was just my friend. I still loved him and always would. I don't look at divorce as failure. Sometimes marriages or relationships just end, and we have to accept that. Despite everything that had happened, it's not like I could just swear off those old feelings. We spoke at least once a day for years, and we still deeply cared for one another. You don't stop loving someone overnight, and I never stopped loving Dee Dee.

When he returned back to the states he tried desperately to win my heart back. We had several dates— we'd go out for dinner and, later, back to his room at the Chelsea Hotel where he now lived full time. He wanted to be intimate, but deep down inside I was afraid that he might have possibly been infected with the AIDS virus, because of all of his drug use, and I just couldn't take that risk. There was still a deep bond between us, but he got bitter towards me at the end when I wouldn't take him back. He told me that it took him a long time to wean himself off of me. Years later he couldn't even hear my name mentioned without becoming emotional and angry. He once told me that whenever he was walking down 8th Street in the city, by Saint Mark's Place, the punks would yell from across the street, "Go back to Vera!"

He told me this himself but refused to go back on his meds, which left me no choice but to move on without him. It never meant that I stopped loving him or caring about him. I just couldn't live with him under these conditions. Now I had to restructure my life and do what was best for me—no matter what. I needed to pick up the broken pieces and make a new life for myself without him.

CHAPTER EIGHTEEN

My Fresh Start

After Dee Dee and I split, I had gotten a job working in real estate as a property manager in Jamaica, Queens. It wasn't great, but I needed to work and that was a start in the right direction. Times were tough and on top of everything else I still had those damn headaches. Dee Dee went abroad to Germany, then Amsterdam, and then London. He always called me from wherever he was and wanted to know how I was doing, and told me to call Ira, his accountant, if I needed anything. I always told him to just take care of himself. I was determined to be self-sufficient and keep my pride. While Dee Dee was living in a flat in London, he had given me the phone number of the nice young couple who lived upstairs from him—so that I could reach him if I needed to. I called once and spoke to his neighbors, who were very kind and friendly, and left a message for Dee Dee to call me back. He called me a couple of days later, asking why I hadn't called him back. I told him I *did* return his call and left a message with his neighbors, who for some reason did not convey my message to him.

When he heard that I had called, and he had not been told, he went ballistic. I later found out that he went and purchased some black paint and painted the stairs leading up to their apartment. When they came home later that night from work, they walked up the stairs in the dark and tracked all the wet black paint into their apartment! I know this to be true because Dee Dee told me he did it. Then the neighbor's wife called me to complain about the horrible thing he had done. What could I say? This was Dee Dee off his medications, and no one would go unpunished—no one.

Christmas was a few days away, and the holidays had always been a special time of year for us. Even though I didn't have any money, I went out and bought Dee Dee some really cool clothes. I bought him a great jacket from Trash and Vaudeville on St. Mark's Place. I also bought him some sweatshirts and jeans and some other warm clothes because he didn't have much. I don't know what he did with all the clothes he had, but he had nothing for the winter. I wrapped everything up with Christmas paper and fancy bows, and since he didn't have a phone, I drove to the city with my sister Linda to surprise him with all the gifts. I knew how much he loved presents and thought that this would make him really happy. I also missed him and especially at that time of year, as it was more emotional for me to be without him. We ventured up five flights of stairs carrying several shopping bags full of gifts. I was hoping he would be home, because I knew this would mean a lot to him. I wanted him to know that he was still loved and someone still cared for him. I wanted nothing more than to overcome the challenges we'd faced since our separation. But that was not to be.

When I finally knocked on his door, he opened it and was quite shocked to see me. I told him I had bought him some Christmas presents that I knew he would love. When he saw me, he became flustered and overwhelmed. He told me there were several people in his living room, homeless people from the park nearby, and I could see the needles and cooking spoons and straps on the kitchen table behind him from the door. My timing could not have been worse—I had come just when they were about to shoot up. My heart just dropped to the floor, and I had a pit in my stomach that made me feel like throwing up. Once again, I had been duped. I gave him the three shopping bags full of goodies and, even though I had been invited in, the scene was not only what I had not expected to find but uncomfortable for me as well. I left there more depressed than ever and realized that he was who he was, and leopards do not change their spots. It was clear to me then that I was still hoping for something that was never going to happen. I realized that I had to let go once and for all, or he would drag me down with him. He tried to change, but eventually the demons within and self-destructiveness finally won him over. I was completely numb by now. I couldn't even cry; I couldn't feel anything. I was sick to my stomach with grief. To this day, I carry the emotional scars from living in an abusive relationship. I don't believe it ever leaves you. To this very day I still flinch at the raise of a hand. It's an automatic and spontaneous response that will stay with me for life.

It had been a while since Dee Dee had quit the Ramones, but every night, after being at work all day long, he would call me just as I was getting in the door. Every night it was a new drama to deal with, but once he proceeded to tell me that he wanted to kill Johnny Ramone. I would talk to him for hours. "Let it go," I would tell him. Killing John would not solve his problems. He would pay the ultimate price and spend the rest of his life in jail, and for what? "What would you gain from this?" I asked him. "You would only be fucking yourself and ruining your own life. Killing Johnny Ramone is not the answer to your problems!" Finally I talked him out of it. I could tell his disease was progressing, which truly concerned me.

The following week he'd call me again, only this time he would announce that he wanted to kill Joey Ramone. Again, I had to talk him out of it, telling him that he must let go of the hostility and hatred. Killing anyone was not the answer! Again, I begged him to go back on his medications, but he was more adamant than ever and that was not up for discussion.

Not too much later, around 1992, he was served with my divorce papers, and he totally freaked out. I feared for my own safety at this time, and I worried that I might become his next victim. It was winter and dark outside. I would drive around the block several times every night before coming home from work, just to make sure he wasn't hiding in the bushes or squatting behind a parked car. I eventually moved to a new apartment, and even there I felt I could be in danger of being stalked or gunned down. It was a horrible feeling, and I knew that the only recourse I had was to leave New York state, where I had lived for almost forty years. It was time to leave and proceed with my new life, in a new place and with a new beginning. I could no longer live in fear.

Before my move, I met a terrific new guy named Kenny. We both had visited my parents in Florida during the Christmas of 1993. It was a very enjoyable trip, and by spring we were already making plans to move there by the end of the summer. It was going to be a very different life for me. I was still having headaches and was diagnosed with depression, but that did not deter Kenny. He assured me that I could count on him, and he would not let me down; he would be there for me. I wanted to be happy and felt it was a waste of time being angry about what had happened in the past. Feeling sorry for myself was not helping me move forward with my life. Still, I just couldn't give my broken heart again to anyone, as much as I wanted to. It literally took me years!

Each day is one you won't get back, and this was going to be a fresh start for me in a new place, with new friends and a new life. This was going to be my new beginning, and I left the state without telling Dee Dee, which made him more angry and hostile than he already was. After moving to Florida I called him and told him where I was. He got totally freaked out and angry, saying I had abandoned him! His illness was getting worse with each passing year and progressing at an alarming rate. He informed me that his mother had also relocated to Florida, not far from me. *I wonder why?*

Everyone was still his enemy, and he was always the victim. Nothing had really changed except that he sounded worse with every conversation we had. He was still angry that I had left the state! He couldn't believe that I could do such a thing. I had to leave for my own safety and for my sanity. For once I decided to put myself first, because he was bringing me down with him and that was unacceptable. Definitely only I could make the changes for my survival. I was still experiencing those awful headaches. Would they ever go away? I had thought that by moving out of New York my mental health would improve, and my headaches would go away. Boy was I wrong! I was always fatigued and decided to concentrate on getting my health back. I was totally drained. I felt physically and emotionally shot. It was going to take time to feel better and building up my immune system was not going to be an easy task.

I remarried after living with Kenny for five years; I really wanted to make sure that I knew the man I was planning to spend the rest of my life with. We tied the knot five months after my divorce was final. There was a stipulation in my divorce decree that stated specifically that neither one of us would talk to the public or do interviews about our past relationship, because Dee Dee was saying such hurtful and untrue things, and I could not take any more lies and humiliation. I had been through enough, and I could not endure any more torture. He became very bitter over the breakup, even though he initiated it. I just couldn't take that anymore, so there was a stipulation written into our divorce decree that said he was not allowed to talk about me or our relationship in his book.

Financially, things could not be worse, and I was forced to file for bankruptcy after moving to Florida in 1993—two years prior to my final divorce. I had no choice. I was mentally and emotionally shot! It took me ten years to reestablish my credit. A year after I remarried, in 1996, I heard that Dee Dee had also gotten married to a much younger girl. I was happy that he'd found a nice girl to settle down with and that he wasn't alone. Being alone was not a good thing for him, and having a new wife would keep him entertained and focused. I was glad that he found someone to spend his life with and that he had also moved on, which was a good thing.

We lost contact after he moved to Los Angeles. I was genuinely happy for him and hoped that relocating to L.A. would be a new beginning for him as well. I wished him the best and hoped that he was finally happy with his new life. He had left the Ramones seven years earlier, and as I'd said before in an interview, I always believed that Joey was the heart of the group, Dee Dee was the soul, and John was the brains. Tommy was the intellectual. And if you couldn't relate to one of the original Ramones, don't worry: Marky, Richie, and C.J. were there too!

Even though the Ramones broke up around 1995, there would never be another band like them. They were the original punk rockers and are considered to be one of the seven most influential bands of all time. They were legends in their own time!

CHAPTER NINETEEN

Till Death Do Us Part

Within three months after the Ramones' induction into the Rock and Roll Hall of Fame, Dee Dee died of an overdose on June 5, 2002. I remember being at work when my sister drove to see me in the middle of the afternoon. I was surprised to see her and wondered what she was doing, visiting me in the middle of the day. I knew she worked in West Palm Beach, which was an hour away. She greeted me and asked me if she could see me outside for a minute for some privacy. It was totally out of character for her to come to my workplace, and I immediately followed her outside, not having a clue what it was all about. She said that she didn't want me to hear it on the news on my way home from work in the car. Then she told me Dee Dee had passed away the previous evening and was found dead—apparently of an overdose—in his apartment by his wife Barbara when she came home from work. I screamed, "No! No! No! Not my Dee Dee! You're wrong! This can't be true! There must be some mistake! He doesn't do heroin anymore!" But there was no mistake. It was true.

Words cannot express how I felt when I heard those words. Our whole life together flashed across my mind like some kind of movie. It was the last thing I expected to hear. My heart went out to Barbara, knowing how she must have felt when she walked through that door. I had dreaded hearing those exact words throughout my whole life. I literally fell apart and could not be consoled. I was numb with grief. My sister drove me home from work, and my boss Chris told me to do whatever I needed to do. He knew how hard this was for me.

When I finally got home that evening, it was all over the news, with Dee Dee's picture and the dates September 18, 1952 to June 5, 2002, R.I.P. I knew I had to accept the truth, but how could this happen? Why now? I assumed that he had finally beat all his demons and found happiness and contentment at this point in his life. I guess I was mistaken. I had hoped, after all this time, that he had made it past the most dangerous time in his life. If he was still engaging in those kinds of activities at fifty years old, one can only imagine what a handful he was in his 20s and 30s. I don't know how we both survived those years!

Even though many years had passed since we had both moved on and remarried, we always had a strong bond, even though his last years were filled with much anger and bitterness about the past. I called his mother, Toni, that night. She was living in Delray, Florida, a little more than one hour from me. We had not spoken in ten years. When she picked up the phone and heard my voice, we both just cried. Our Dee Dee was gone! We knew all too well the pain and loss that Barbara was going through, and our hearts and prayers were with her. Toni expressed her desire to go to California to say good-bye to her only son. She loved him very much. I also wanted to pay my last respects and say good-bye.

Many things were left unsaid between Dee Dee and me, and we never resolved our differences. We parted with heavy hearts and much bitterness. Still, I needed to bid my final farewell, not just for my sake but also to help his mother see her son for the last time. I called Barbara that very night and expressed my deep condolences and asked her if it would be all right for his mother and I to come to L.A. and pay our last respects to Dee Dee. I told her that I would totally understand if she said no, but she didn't hesitate. I will always be grateful to her for that.

Barbara was very gracious and told me we would be welcome, but we would need to make our own provisions as she was very busy making all the arrangements for the funeral and burial. I completely understood. His mother and I landed at LAX airport after a ten-hour flight at about 11:30 pm. We were met at the airport by Barbara herself, Gary Kurfirst's assistant, and Barbara's best friend, Leah. It was the first time I had actually met Barbara, and we embraced each other tightly and cried. The loss was felt not only by us but by his close friends, too, as well as his fans all over the world. Our beloved Dee Dee was gone forever. Hopefully he was finally at peace with himself. Some people suspected suicide, but I seriously had my doubts. I knew him better than that.

My cousin Luba Mason Blades was kind enough to allow Toni and me to stay at her home while funeral arrangements were being made. Two days later, his mother and I were allowed to have a private viewing after they prepared his body for the burial, which was set for the following morning at the Hollywood Forever Cemetery. His mother went in first to pay her last respects and to say good-bye to her son. They didn't see each other much in those last few years, and they seldom spoke to each other. Dee Dee was mad at the whole world in his last years. Toni left there with tears flowing. Next it was my turn. I looked down at his lifeless body. He was dressed in a beautiful suit, the one he wore to the Rock and Roll Hall of Fame, and he looked good. He looked as though he was sleeping. I remember telling him how sorry I was at the way things had ended between us, but that I had never stopped loving him and I never would. I was so disappointed that his life had ended so tragically. After saying my final good-bye and a prayer for him, I took the dolphin ring that he had last given me off my finger and placed it inside his jacket's top-left pocket. "Good-bye my precious Dee Dee. I will never stop loving you, and we shall see each other again. Till next time…." (As I am writing these very words at this moment, today would have been our 29th wedding anniversary. How ironic—tears are rolling down my face once again!)

The following day was Dee Dee's burial. I hadn't gotten much sleep at all the night before, but the day I had dreaded for years had finally arrived. On this day, the reality finally sunk in. My cousin took Toni and me to the cemetery that morning. Immediately I recognized several familiar faces that I had not seen for many years. Arturo Vega was the first person to greet me and hug me, and then there was our good friend Danny Fields. Then I saw and hugged our good friend and Dee Dee's accountant, Ira Herzog. Barbara came over and we embraced. The looks on our faces said it all. Also in attendance were people that I had not seen for many years: Tommy Ramone, Daniel Rey, Linda and Johnny Ramone, and Arthur Kane (formerly of the New York Dolls). CJ Ramone was there, and he spoke at the eulogy as did many others who bid their final farewell to their friend Dee Dee Ramone.

As the casket was carried in front of us by the pallbearers, Barbara stood in the middle, with Toni on her right and me on Barbara's left. The three of us walked behind the casket following our beloved, dear Dee Dee. Behind us was a large crowd that consisted of longtime friends and people he had befriended during the course of many years: people who loved him and people whose lives he had touched; people who will never forget him for his kindness, his great sense of humor, his loyalty, and artistic creativity, as well as his craziness. Dee Dee was also very lovable, and he could get away with murder, but this was a part of his charm and his unique and wonderful personality.

After several speakers gave the eulogy, his casket was placed into his new home in the ground under a beautiful oak tree. One by one, the people present picked up a rose and threw it on top of his casket. I remember seeing Barbara trembling and shaking. I knew exactly what she must have been feeling at that moment. I prayed for her as well. She was too young to become a widow and didn't deserve this. She was scared, and I was scared for her too. She encouraged me to go up and throw my rose onto his casket like the others. When I did, it was so final. This was the end, and I was filled with sadness, as tears flowed down my face. Barbara was born in 1978, the year Dee Dee and I were married. We lived in a whole different world before she met him, but neither she nor I had any ill feelings toward one another. On the contrary, I was happy for him. I was happy that he had finally found someone with whom to share those last years of his life so he wasn't alone anymore. He hated being alone!

After the ceremony was over there wasn't much left to say, and Toni and I departed and prepared for our return back to Florida. It was a long and very sad trip home for the both of us. We reminisced about his lovable and crazy ways and both agreed that he would always be loved and missed, not just by us but by all the people whose hearts he had touched throughout his years here. He would also be missed by his many devoted and loyal fans all over the world. The world will never see another Dee Dee Ramone. He was one of those special souls that come around only once in a lifetime. He was the second Ramone to have passed in a little over a year, and I knew that Johnny was also very sick. I prayed for him that day as well. After Dee Dee's death, Barbara and I spoke several times and shared many stories about the Dee Dee we both knew and loved. Sometimes we talked for hours at a time. We have always remained on good terms.

It was mid-September 2004, when my close friend Linda Ramone called me and told me Johnny had taken a turn for the worse. I spoke to her regularly, and she always kept me informed. She was witnessing his steady decline, even though Johnny had fought for such a long, hard time. In the end, his fate was sealed, and he took his place in heaven beside his brothers. Even though they were never actually related, they all shared the same fictitious last time, Ramone, and spent more time together than most biological brothers.

After Johnny and Linda had moved to Los Angeles from New York, they experienced a much different life. Johnny had mellowed out quite a bit by then and had numerous celebrity friends. They were just beginning to enjoy their new life when Johnny was diagnosed with prostate cancer. This was a terrible blow, but they had no choice but to deal with it. Johnny became a much nicer person in his last years and could actually be quite pleasant when he liked someone, and when he wanted to. There were two very opposite sides to him for those of us who knew him well. After many years, Johnny and I had come to terms with our differences. It was all a long time ago, and he was quite friendly to me when I would call Linda. Kenny and I even went to Disney World in Orlando with them when they came to Florida for a visit. We all actually got along great and have some nice memories of those times.

When I heard Johnny had passed, I sent my condolences and shared my grief with Linda. To lose a loved one is never easy, even though they had both known for a long time that Johnny was living on borrowed time. One is never prepared for the worst. We could not understand why all three of them had been taken away within barely a year of one another. Why? They were so young. Was this the curse of the Ramones that the crazy preacher had ranted about so many years ago? Or was this just a mere coincidence? The three Ramones were gone, and the world will never see another Joey, Dee Dee, or Johnny again. The only Ramones reunion there will ever be will be up in heaven. I can hear them playing now: 1-2-3-4!

I've heard references made to the Ramones as being "Johnny's band." I would like to correct that by stating that they were all equally important members, and each had their own role in making the Ramones a unit. Combined, they became one of the most influential bands in rock and roll history. Without songwriters and singers there would be no albums to record—certainly there would be no music for their fans to listen to. So, well-deserved credit must be given equally to each of the Ramones. To do otherwise would be sacrilegious.

In 2007, the tragic death of Linda Stein shocked and overwhelmed me with grief. She had been killed in her high-security Fifth Avenue apartment. How could anyone do something so horrible? Within a short period of time it was discovered that Linda had been killed by her own personal assistant, a woman. Once again, I thought to myself, *Was this part of the Ramones' Curse?* I have to question if there even are such things as curses, but how else does one explain all of these tragic deaths? A coincidence? Maybe. But what if it they're not? Who's the next victim? My gut feeling tells me this is not over, although I hope to God I'm wrong. I have wonderful memories of Linda in the early days when she co-managed the Ramones with Danny Fields. She was feisty, but if she liked you, she was also nice and a lot of fun. We had many girl chats in our hotel rooms while the boys did sound checks before the shows. On my very first tour of England, she was the first one to take me shopping in the trendy area of Kings Road and to Harrods department store. I have wonderful memories of her, and she will be missed by many. Most of all, I remember her being pregnant with her first child, Mandy. During her pregnancy she constantly craved Cool Whip and would indulge herself by eating the whole tub! Her hormones were definitely peaking—something a Ramone would never understand about a pregnant woman—and the boys would just look at her with puzzled grins.

I would also like to acknowledge the sudden passing of the Ramones' longtime manager of over seventeen years, Gary Kurfirst, in mid-January of 2009. Like the Ramones, Gary had also attended Forest Hills High School, and in many ways the band looked up to him as a big brother. Even from an early age, Gary was already a pioneer. He managed rock acts like Leslie West and Mountain while Joey, Johnny, Dee Dee, and Tommy were skipping school and only dreaming of becoming rock stars. Gary was a brilliant businessman and had a knack for picking unique bands that were on the cutting edge and stood out based on their originality.

Among the many other bands whose careers he managed were acts like the Talking Heads, Blondie, the B 52's, Eurythmics, Big Audio Dynamite, and Jane's Addiction. Gary was a tremendous inspiration to Dee Dee and encouraged him to keep writing music. Dee Dee looked up to Gary and respected him and never wanted to let him down. He was one of the few people that Dee Dee would listen to. Gary also urged Dee Dee to stick to his sobriety and was always there for both of us during many troubled times. He was not just a business manager. He truly cared about us and helped out in any way he could.

My heart and deepest condolences go out to his lovely wife Phyllis, who was his childhood sweetheart since they were fourteen years old, his children Lindsey and Josh, his mom Joan, and his entire extended family. Gary was an amazing manager, husband, father, grandfather, and friend and leaves a truly admirable legacy behind that is respected by all of us who knew him. We are profoundly saddened by the loss of this extraordinary man and feel privileged to have known him. He will be greatly missed.

Six weeks after Johnny's death, I was admitted to the hospital for some routine tests. I told my husband Kenny that my headaches were worse than ever. I was feeling nauseous all the time now and could barely walk around the house without holding on to the walls. My head was spinning. *What was happening?* I had no explanation, and I told him I was really scared. He assured me that whatever it was, we would face it together! "But what about my job? You? My dog? Who was gonna take care of everything if I wasn't well?" By this point, my boss Chris was not just my boss; he had become like a brother to me. Over the many years we had worked together, he knew me well and told me to just take care of myself and not worry about my job.

After a battery of horrible tests that all came back negative, my doctor told me I could go home. Hallelujah!

"But before I go, Doc," I asked, "Can you give me something for my sinus infection and headache?"

"Of course," he replied, and as he started to write out a prescription for me, he looked up and asked if I would mind staying one more day. He said he would like to have a brain MRI done. I rolled my eyes at him as I looked at Kenny, and I asked the doctor if this was really necessary. It was Kenny who interjected and said, "What the hell. You've had every other test done! What's one more?"

"O.K.," I said, "But can I go home tomorrow?"

"Yes, you can."

I had the brain MRI taken that very afternoon, and by 6:00 p.m. my doctor was back in my room.

"Hi, Doc!" I smiled. "What are you doing here again so soon?" I had just seen him four hours earlier and was not expecting to see him again until the next day at the very earliest. He proceeded to sit at the edge of my bed. As he looked at my smiling face he began to tell me that the brain MRI I had taken two hours prior showed that I had multiple tumors on the brain and that a neurologist would be doing some additional testing.

"Doctor, what are you telling me? Are you saying that I have brain cancer?"

He nodded his head, and I could feel my blood pressure rise to the ceiling within seconds. I sat there in sheer disbelief and completely numb. I couldn't even comprehend what he said afterwards. Everything sounded like a blur. This was the last thing I expected to hear. Again I thought to myself, was this the continuation of the Ramones' Curse that we had all witnessed a long time ago. *Was I its next victim?*

I remained hospitalized for the next three months, and five neurosurgeons later, Dr. Jacques Morcos, the professor of Neurology at the University of Miami at Jackson Memorial Hospital, finally agreed to remove the brain tumor that was leaning on my brain stem and spinal cord. There were no promises made; the doctors made sure I knew what the consequences could be. Prior to the operation, Ken and I were advised to get all our affairs in order and to prepare for the worst. The operation was done as soon as possible—Dr. Morcos assured me that after having spent the last three months in the hospital, I would not have survived one more week! Time was not an option for me, and I signed the necessary papers and gave my consent for the surgery, which was scheduled for the following morning. What was meant to be would be.

I did survive this life-changing experience. Still, in many ways my breakup with Dee Dee was even more painful than the brain surgery. The heart takes much longer to heal than the actual physical healing itself. The worst was over, even though the doctors informed me that I still had several brain tumors left. The good news was that they were benign for now, and they were slow-growing. They said I'd probably had them for at least fifteen years. After years of being treated for allergies, sinus infections, stress, and depression, I finally knew what had caused my "headaches"! I went home and knew the healing process was going to be long and tedious. I've never been the same since the operation, and the vertigo will most likely stay with me for the rest of my life. However, one learns to adjust and take it one day at a time. I look forward to the future, however long that may be.

Experiencing something like this truly humbles you and makes you appreciate each and every day that you are given. Life is precious—it is a gift that can be taken away in the blink of an eye. I learned that I am a lot stronger than I thought I was, and what doesn't kill you will only make you stronger in the long run. You don't live life and not know heartache, sorrow, and pain. Few are lucky enough to find true love once, let alone twice, in one lifetime. I consider myself very lucky despite everything I've been through.

* * *

It had been quite some time since I last spoke with Lene Leigh (wife of Mickey Leigh, Joey Ramones' brother). I had been told by my agent Aime, that Lene had found this incredible lady, Linda Drake, and I might want to contact her to set up a reading where she could "channel" Dee Dee's spirit. Ironically, Aime was also Linda Drake's agent at this time and was helping her promote her book that had just been released. I was told that Linda might be able to give me the closure I had been looking for with Dee Dee and the various unresolved issues which had left me with much sadness and a heavy heart throughout all these years.

Even though Linda Drake was on tour promoting her book *Reaching Through the Veil to Heal,* she agreed to a reading within three days of my contacting her. To my surprise, she called me back just five minutes later, saying that Dee Dee had come through to her, and he was very anxious to speak with me! I was completely elated, and she agreed to come to my house the very next morning at 11:00 am. It was so ironic that she just happened to be in Orlando and was only two hours from my home.

I displayed all his Dee Dee King memorabilia, pictures, and personal items on the dining room table. Linda told me that he kept telling her he was the King the whole ride down, but this did not make any sense to her until she walked into my house and saw all the Dee Dee King stuff I had displayed. The moment she walked in, she said, "So that's what he meant when he kept saying he was the King!" It wasn't long before she started to channel Dee Dee to me through her. She had never heard of Dee Dee or the Ramones. She knew nothing about him or me or our history. However, she described his personality to a tee. She told me personal things that only he and I knew and told me that he took full responsibility for our breakup. He said it was all his fault; the drugs were his demons, and he couldn't shake them. He knew he had drained me of all my energy over the years, and there was just nothing I had left to give. It was a matter of survival—mine—and he loved me so much he had to let me go.

This woman knew nothing of my previous life, why we broke up, or even his eventual overdose, so the next thing she told me really blew my head! To my surprise, she told me that I had died on the operating table and that Dee Dee met me on the other side. He told me it was not my time yet, that I had much work left to do, and with that she said he gave me a hug and sent me back. He said when my time comes, he will be there waiting for me and will walk me through to the other side. This was very comforting for me to hear. I told Linda I had no recall of this, and she said that it was my choice not to. I had never mentioned the operation to her during our phone conversation, and there was no way this woman could have known that two years earlier I had had a so-called inoperable brain tumor removed and that I had flat-lined on that operating table.

To this day, Dr. Morcos calls me his miracle patient whenever he sees me for my post-op visits. But Kenny and I did not tell anyone, even my own parents and extended family members, that I had flat-lined! We felt there was no reason to alarm everyone even more and decided to keep this private for obvious and personal reasons. *How could Linda possibly know this?* Not even my own family knew.

After almost three hours of the reading, she asked me to sit on a chair in the middle of the room. She said she was going to perform a healing of the hands on me. I had no idea what this was all about but did as I was told and sat down on the chair that she pulled out for me. Linda's hands never actually touched my head, and after she held her hands over my head for several minutes, I still didn't feel anything unusual. I was feeling quite skeptical actually. At least five minutes had passed when I started to feel like there were hundred of ants crawling under my scalp. This continued for at least twenty minutes, and the heat of the energy was undeniable. After the healing, the hair on my head was standing up from the static energy!

I want to express my gratitude to Lene Leigh for originally finding Linda Drake. The quality of my life has not been this good for many years, and I am very appreciative to her for that. The entire experience with Linda Drake was overwhelming, and one I will never forget. She lifted the heaviness and guilt that I had carried within my heart for so many years. I was given several messages on this day from the other side. One was that I should travel to California to participate in a group meeting called "Circle of Love" to help keep the legacy of the Ramones alive. There were several other messages—of a more personal nature—that I've chosen not to discuss at this time. I was also requested by Dee Dee to write this book and tell it how it really was—the good, the bad, and everything in between. He kept saying, "Write the book! Timing is everything!"

Many times I started to write this book and then stopped. It was too painful, and I finally told Kenny, "I'm not going to do this." At that precise moment, Linda Drake called me and after exchanging hellos, she asked, "Vera, are you still writing your book?" I responded, saying it was funny that she mentioned that, because I was just telling Kenny five minutes earlier that I wasn't going to continue writing anymore!

She said, "Dee Dee kept telling me that you must continue. He said you need to finish this book."

It was very eerie, to say the least, but he insisted that I continue. I felt that I had a responsibility to uphold his wishes and somewhat of an obligation to fulfill his request and keep his legacy alive. This is what he wanted, and I hope that I have not disappointed him.

CHAPTER TWENTY

Here Today, Gone Tomorrow: R.I.P. in the Garden of Serenity

Writing this book about my life with Dee Dee Ramone has been an amazing journey. It stirred up many emotions, old feelings, and memories that I thought had long been forgotten. I realize that some things, as well as certain people, are unforgettable. Dee Dee, Joey, and Johnny may be gone, but they have left us with their music and their legacy to continue for many generations to come. Their spirit lives on. *Gabba Gabba Hey!* What they created in their short time here is timeless, and they would want their fans to remember them always.

Dee Dee lived each day as though it were his last. He always created something new and different and left no stone unturned. He was truly a very special soul, and I know that after so many years of pain and struggling with his demons, he's finally in a wonderful place and at peace with himself.

I want him to be remembered not just for his rebellious and self-destructive behavior, but also for his many wonderful qualities, which were abundant. He was fearless, yet sensitive, loving yet defiant. He possessed a wonderful sense of humor and a passion for creativity that few can equal. His deep hearty laugh will always be remembered. His generosity towards others and warm, giving heart will not be forgotten. What he really loved was seeing the joy on the faces of his fans when he played his music for them. That was his greatest gift to us, and the legacy he would want to be remembered by. He was a true punk rocker, but with a lot of heart and soul.

I have chosen, rather than to cry over what I've lost, to smile about what I've had—and I've had a lot. So, for now, my dear Dee Dee, I bid you a final farewell, until we meet again on the "Highest Trails Above."

Faithfully Yours Forever,

"Baby Doll"

DEE DEE RAMONE

SEPTEMBER 18, 1951 - JUNE 5, 2002

R.I.P. We miss you!!
1-2-3-4!!
Gabba Gabba Hey!

"Faithfully Yours"

> faithfuly youre forever
>
> I didn't ask for anything
> anything from you
> you took me for granted
> and broke my heart in too
> but I didn't drown
> myself in the pain
> I comforted my heart
> with a walk in the rain
>
> I remember one september day
> I waited for the mail
> but all my prayers
> were to no avail
> your just so selfish
> but what done is done
> and all the lonelyness
> is something I don't wellcome
>
> I'll be faithfully yours forever
> youll be in my memory
> I hope that you never
> forget about me

Music and lyrics by Dee Dee Ramone and Daniel Ray 1989 - Never released.

"Faithfully Yours" continued.

I am not beggin
to be your friend
or part of your world
cause one precious pearl
as delicate as porcelain
as strong as the wind
will always be happen
she never gets burned again

I be faithfuly yours forever
youll be in my memory
I hope that you never
forget about me

I'll be faithfuly yours forever
your in my memory
I'll be faithfuly yours forever
and this I garrentee
I'll be faithfuly yours forever
and dont forget about me
I'll love you forever faithfuly

"Highest Trails Above"

Music and lyrics by Dee Dee Ramone
Song recorded by the Ramones.

ACKNOWLEDGMENTS

When I first began pondering the idea of *Poisoned Heart* becoming a reality, over a year and a half ago, I knew there was a lot to do, but I had no idea how many people it would take to complete this task. This has been a labor of love in every sense of the word, and I'd like to thank everyone who helped me tell my story.

First and foremost I would like to thank Michael Viner and Henrietta Tiefenthaler at Phoenix Books for giving me a chance and believing in my book's potential.

Special thanks to Dan Smetanka for his brilliant and ingenious vision and direction for my book.

To my editor Alina Poniewaz, you have been a joy to work with and made this whole editing process as easy as possible and still let me keep true to my heart so that my voice could be heard.

The entire staff at Phoenix Books for working so diligently and hard to make my book the best it could be— last but certainly not least many thanks to my publicist Brian Gross—I thank you all.

I would like to thank my dear, close friend, confidant, and advisor Chad Pate for his wisdom and making me believe in myself and that I could make this possible.

Jamielyn Ayres for her countless hours condensing twenty years worth of notes and diaries, and for typing my manuscript and being flexible and available to work around my good and bad days, whenever I needed her.

My agent and representative Aime McCrory and her husband Steve for their friendship, hard work, and dedication and for never giving up on me and sticking by me through the tough times. I couldn't have made it without you, thank you.

My mentor and friend for life, David Dalton, for your guidance and utmost support. To Bob Gruen, my friend for thirty-plus years, who urged me four years ago to put together this memoir. Keith Green who believed in my project from the beginning and who has become a close, dear friend. To my lawyer Mark S. Corrinet—no words can express my gratitude for all your invaluable advice and help. Alexander P. Hartnett for your personal interest and help. Many thanks to Frank Rose.

To George Bennett, your friendship and advice I will treasure for life. My dear friend Jim Bessman, you've been wonderful, and I will always remember your kind words and encouragement. Thank you.

I'd like to thank my dear friends Ellen and David MacArthur, Mary Jane and Leo Ambrogi and their son, the future rockstar, "Lil Leo." Angela Galetta, Lene and Mickey Leigh (Joey Ramones brother and sister-in-law), Legs McNeil, Suzie Springman, Linda Drake, Kathy Bucheit, Nicole Blevin, Phyllis Kurfirst, Katie Elliott, and Arturo Vega. To Monte A. Melnick, for always being there for me when I needed you most and never letting me down during all those tumultuous times—thank you for always being my friend and literally saving my life!

Warmest thanks to good pals Tina Weymouth and Chris Frantz of Talking Heads and TomTom Club for their continued friendship and wonderful foreword to my book, and to Michael Musto Lenny Kaye and Daniel Rey.

Most of all, special thanks to my parents, John and Rose Boldis, my sisters and brothers-in-law—Sonja and Tony Nienstedt, and Linda and Matthew Pancari—my sister Ellen Boldis, and my brother and sister-in-law, John and Liz Boldis. To my awesome nephews T.J., Eric and Michael, and my nieces, Allison and Lauren. To my cousin Luba Mason Blades for her support. My sister-in-law Pamela Hess, for her relentless "You can do this" phrase that I can still hear in my head.

Last but certainly not least, my mother-in-law always, Toni Colvin (Dee Dee's mom)—time cannot erase the bond we share. The words "thank you" are not enough for living this with me. Without your love and support throughout all these years and rough times, I don't know how I could have "survived."

To my sweet, lovable dog "Schatzee," for never leaving my side for hours on end. I will miss you terribly and remember your sweet face with tears in my eyes.

For my wonderful husband Kenny, there are no words that can be said. You have been sent to me by an angel, and if it were not for you I would not be here today. We both know that. Thank you for letting me do what I needed to do, while you had to endure all those frozen dinners. I love you.

PHOTO CREDITS

I would like to thank the photographers for the wonderful photos that were provided to me for this book. The photographs enhanced the chapters and allowed the reader to fully envision the stories depicted.

My deepest thanks to: George Bennett, Keith Green, Bob Gruen, Roberta Bayley, Eileen Polk, Kees Tabak, Jenny Lens, Clay Holden, Ian Harper, Ron Ross, Godlis, Lindell Tate, Jimmy Marino, Arturo Vega, Frank Granada, Angela Galetta, Daniel Rey, Shawn Chadwick, Fernando Guerrero and Dot Stein.

www.veraramoneking.com